1

FACTS

Liverpool

First published in Great Britain in ...

by X xxxx Publishing

www.xxxxpublishing.com

Kindle Publishing is a trading name of X Wenlock Co., xxx

Copyright © ... xxxx 20xx, xxxx, Harper/Collins Publishing

ISBN 978-1-908724-13-7

Printed by xxx, Hampton ...

First published in Great Britain in 2014
by Wymer Publishing
www.wymerpublishing.co.uk
Wymer Publishing is a trading name of Wymer (UK) Ltd

ISBN 978-1-908724-13-7

Edited by Jerry Bloom.

Typeset by Andy Francis.
Printed and bound by Clays, Bungay, Suffolk.

A catalogue record for this book is available from the British Library.

Cover design by Andy Francis.
Sketches by Becky Welton. © 2013.

100 FACTS

Liverpool

Steve Horton

WP
WYMER
PUBLISHING
Bedford, England

100 FACTS

Liverpool

Steve Horton

WP

1892
LIVERPOOL FOUNDED
AFTER EVERTON LEAVE ANFIELD

Liverpool's origins lay in disagreements between Everton FC and John Houlding, the leaseholder of Anfield.

Everton were formed in 1878 and started playing at Anfield in 1884, winning their first Football League Championship in 1891. However a dispute arose in January 1892 when Houlding, who had loaned Everton money to make improvements to the ground, asked for more rent.

Everton's shareholders, who were also unhappy that Houlding supplied all the refreshments for the ground from his Sandon pub, refused to agree to an increase and moved to a patch of land on the other side of Stanley Park named Mere Green, which became known as Goodison Park. Houlding was now left with a football ground but no club so along with some Everton officials who remained loyal to him, formed Liverpool FC on 3rd June 1892.

The club applied to join the 2nd Division of the Football League but this was rejected so they joined the Lancashire League instead.

Liverpool's first match in the Lancashire League was on 8th September 1892 when they beat Higher Walton 8-0 in front of only 200 supporters, but word soon spread of the team and in their next league match at Anfield three weeks later, 4,000 watched a 4-0 win against Bury.

1893
FIRST SEASON SUCCESS
BUT THE CUPS ARE STOLEN

Liverpool's first team was put together by John McKenna, one of the Everton officials who had remained loyal to John Houlding and they enjoyed a double success in their first season.

McKenna was from Northern Ireland but had connections in Scotland and recruited over a dozen Scots. This lead to the team becoming known as the 'Team of All the Macs', due to eight of the side that played in 1892-93 having 'Mc' as part of their surname, although one of the goalkeepers Bill McOwen was English. McKenna managed the side along with William Barclay, Everton's former manager who was also a school headmaster.

The club won eleven of their first thirteen games and were champions of the Lancashire League, finishing ahead of Blackpool on goal average. They also won the Liverpool Senior Cup, beating Everton 1-0 in the final in front of 10,000 fans at Bootle, although there was disappointment in the Lancashire Senior Cup where they reached the final but lost 2-1 to Bootle.

Unfortunately the two trophies that Liverpool won were stolen from the window of a pawn shop in Paddington where they had been put on display. They were never found and Liverpool had to pay £130 to replace them.

1894
LIVERPOOL BEAT MANCHESTER UNITED TO WIN PROMOTION

After winning the Lancashire League, Liverpool successfully applied to join the Football League and they won promotion in their first season.

Liverpool's admission was at the expense of another local club, Bootle, who had been suffering from financial problems and withdrew from the league. However John McKenna had made the application without telling William Barclay, who was surprised to receive a telegram telling him to go to London and arrange the fixtures for the new season.

On 2nd September 1893 Liverpool played their first game in the 2nd Division, beating Middlesbrough Ironopolis 2-0 away from home, the goals coming from Joe McQue and Malcolm McVean. A week later at Anfield, Lincoln City were beaten 4-0. Liverpool went on to finish the season unbeaten at the top of the table, winning all fourteen of their games at Anfield.

Despite winning the league Liverpool still weren't promoted automatically and had to play a 'test match' against Manchester United, who were then known as Newton Heath and had finished bottom of the 1st Division. Liverpool won 2-0 at Anfield to seal promotion although they would be relegated back to the 2nd Division after just one season in the top flight.

1895
LIVERPOOL'S EXTRA TIME WINNER CANCELLED

When Liverpool played Barnsley St Peters (now Barnsley) away at Oakwell in the 1st round of the FA Cup on 2nd February 1895 they thought they had secured a 2-1 win after extra time, but after protests from the home side a replay was ordered.

At the time Liverpool were battling relegation from the 1st Division while Barnsley were in the Midland League. Malcolm McVean gave Liverpool a 25th minute lead but despite their underdog status Barnsley came back to equalise with ten minutes left.

Despite the protests of Barnsley extra time was played, with Jimmy Ross scoring what he thought was the winning goal in the 113th minute. But at the end of extra time Barnsley officials confronted the referee with rule 17 of the competition, which stated that extra time should only be played if both clubs agree. As such the game was declared a draw and replay arranged at Anfield for 11th February.

The *Liverpool Mercury* predicted that Liverpool would be too strong for Barnsley in the replay and they were right. They were 3-0 up at half time thanks to goals from Thomas Bradshaw, John Drummond and Malcolm McVean. Hugh McQueen scored the fourth goal on the hour. Barnsley never gave up hope and tested the Liverpool keeper on a few occasions, but there was never any doubt about the home side's progress to the next round.

In the 2nd round Liverpool faced Nottingham Forest, who they had beaten 5-0 at Anfield in the league a month earlier. But there was to be no repeat this time as the Reds lost 2-0.

1896
LIVERPOOL
SCORE TEN

On 18th February 1896 Liverpool beat Rotherham Town 10-1 in a 2nd Division match at Anfield, which remains the only time they have scored ten goals in a league game.

After being relegated the previous season, Liverpool were determined to bounce straight back to the 1st Division and going into this match were second in the table, one point behind Manchester City.

Liverpool had won 5-0 at Rotherham earlier in the season and the Yorkshire side had lost nine out of their ten away games but nobody had predicted a result such as this. Despite kicking against the wind in the first half Liverpool were 5-0 up after 23 minutes and it was half an hour before keeper Harry Storer touched the ball.

It was 6-0 at half time and the onslaught continued in the second half, Liverpool scoring twice soon after the restart. Rotherham's goal came when they were 9-0 down and despite pulling everyone back into defence to try and avoid conceding a tenth Jimmy Ross did so late in the game.

The only other times Liverpool have scored ten or more since were in European games against Dundalk in 1969 and Strømsgodset in 1974, and Fulham in a League Cup tie in 1987. At the end of 1895-96 they were promoted again, beating Small Heath (now Birmingham City) and West Bromwich Albion in test matches.

1896
A NEW MANAGER
AND NEW SHIRT COLOUR

After four seasons of playing in blue and white Liverpool changed their shirt colours to red for the 1896-97 season as a new manager was also unveiled.

After winning promotion back to the 1st Division John McKenna moved to a boardroom role, but there was a surprise when Liverpool appointed Tom Watson, who had managed Sunderland to three league championships. Watson doubled his wages by moving to Liverpool and soon implemented changes in respect of the players training routines and diets.

Another area where there was change was in the shirt colours. For the first four years of their existence Liverpool played in blue and white halved shirts, similar to what Blackburn Rovers wear today but from now on they would be wearing red.

Their first appearance under Watson's management and in the new shirts was on 1st September 1896 away to The Wednesday (now Sheffield Wednesday). The Reds won the game 2-1, George Allan scoring both the goals with the *Liverpool Mercury* describing them as looking 'resplendent in their new red shirts'.

1897
FIRST
INTERNATIONAL PLAYER

In March 1897 Frank Becton became the first Liverpool player to play in an international after he was selected to play for England against Wales.

Becton had signed for Liverpool from Preston North End for £100 two years earlier after they refused his request for a pay rise. He made his debut on 25th March 1895, scoring in a 3-2 defeat by Sunderland. The following season he scored 18 goals in 24 appearances as they were promoted back to the 1st Division.

On 29th March 1897 Becton was selected to play for England against Wales in the British Championship at Sheffield United's Bramall Lane ground, making him the first Liverpool player to appear for his country. In front of a crowd of 5,000 England won the game 4-0 although it would be the last time Becton appeared for them.

Becton left Liverpool in October 1898, joining Sheffield United and he later played for Preston again and then Swindon Town. Sadly he died in 1909 of tuberculosis aged just 36.

1901
FIRST
LEAGUE TITLE

In 1900-01 Liverpool were crowned 1st Division champions for the first time.

After looking out of the title race in February, they went on a run of nine wins in eleven games to draw level on points with leaders Sunderland, who completed their fixtures before Liverpool's last game away to West Bromwich Albion. Liverpool went to The Hawthorns knowing that a draw against a team that had already been relegated would be enough to clinch the title.

It was a dismal Monday afternoon and there were less than 2,000 fans in the ground when the game kicked off, with the Reds looking for victory rather than settle for the draw. Midway through the half Sam Raybould's shot was only parried by Albion keeper Joe Reader and John Walker smashed the ball into the net. Albion sought to restore some pride and bombarded the Liverpool goal in the second half but the resolute defence held on.

After the game the Reds were presented with the championship trophy before returning to Liverpool by train, where they were met by thousands of fans at Central Station. A band played The Conquering Hero as the players were carried shoulder high, although nobody tried to lift larger than life boss Tom Watson.

1904
OLDEST
DEBUTANT

In September 1904 Ned Doig made his first appearance for Liverpool aged 37 years 307 days, making him older on his Liverpool debut than most players were on retirement.

Doig had played over 400 games for Sunderland, where Liverpool manager Tom Watson had been his boss in the early 1890s. After the Reds were relegated to the 2nd Division at the end of 1903-04, Watson spent £150 to bring his old keeper to Anfield and it proved to be an inspired signing.

Doig's debut was on the opening day of the season, when the Reds beat Burton United 2-0 and he went on to play in all that season's league games. He conceded just 25 goals in 34 matches as Liverpool again won promotion back to the 1st Division at the first attempt.

Despite starting the 1905-06 season as first choice keeper, Doig lost his place after eight games to Sam Hardy. He went on to play just nine more games for the club, the last of which was in a 3-1 defeat at Newcastle United in April 1908. He was 41 years 165 days old in that game, a record that has not been beaten.

Doig was released by the club soon afterwards and he went on playing for two more years with St Helens Recs in the Lancashire League.

1906
SECOND
LEAGUE CHAMPIONSHIP

In 1906 Liverpool won the Football League Championship for the second time as they became the first club to win promotion and then become 1st Division champions in successive seasons.

Despite the eventual success the Reds started the season badly, losing their first three games. However they soon turned the corner and went on an eleven game unbeaten run between October and December.

Essentially the team was the same that had won promotion, except for Sam Hardy replacing Ned Doig in goal and Joe Hewitt, a centre forward signed from Sunderland in January 1904, being handed a regular place in the team. Hewitt's 24 goals were a crucial factor in Liverpool winning the title that season, the first time that twenty clubs played in the top flight.

On Easter Monday Liverpool, backed by 1,000 supporters, travelled to Bolton Wanderers knowing a win would clinch the title. Although they lost 3-2, Preston North End's defeat at Sunderland meant that the Reds could not be caught at the top of the table with one game remaining.

Sadly Liverpool's hopes of doing a double that season were dashed by neighbours Everton, who beat them 2-0 in the FA Cup semi-final at Villa Park. As a reward for winning the championship though, the players were taken on a trip to Paris.

1908
FIRST
OLYMPIAN PLAYER

The first Liverpool player to appear in the Olympic Games was Arthur Berry, who won a gold medal with Great Britain in 1908.

Berry was the son of Chairman Edwin Berry and signed as an amateur in 1906, making just three league appearances for the club between then and 1909. Part of the reason for this was that he was also studying law at Oxford University and whilst playing for their football team he was called up to represent Great Britain in the Olympics of 1908, which were held in London.

In the quarter-final Berry scored one of the goals in Great Britain's 12-1 win over Sweden. They then beat the Netherlands 4-0 in the semi-final before winning 2-0 against Denmark in the gold medal match at the White City Stadium, which was the main stadium for the games.

Berry, along with Joe Dines (who joined from Ilford and made just one appearance for the club in 1912-13), was again representing Great Britain in the 1912 Olympics in Stockholm. This time they beat Hungary and Finland on their way to another gold medal match with Denmark, which Great Britain won 4-2.

After brief spells with Fulham and Everton, Berry made one more appearance for Liverpool in 1912-13 before retiring from football, joining his father's law firm. Berry and Dines both fought in the First World War, with Dines being killed in action in France in 1918.

1909
REMARKABLE
6-5 VICTORY

On 4th December 1909 Liverpool were involved in an amazing game against Newcastle United when they came from 5-2 down to win 6-5.

Liverpool had struggled since winning the title in 1906 and in 1908-09 they avoided relegation by just two points while Newcastle had finished as champions.

However before this game the Reds were in fifth place, ahead of Newcastle on goal average and although a close scoreline may have been predicted, nobody thought the game would evolve as it did.

Newcastle attacked Liverpool from the kick off and were 1-0 up after a minute when Sam Hardy misjudged a cross and Jimmy Howie headed into an empty net. Although Jim Stewart soon levelled, Newcastle took command and by half time Albert Shepherd had scored four times as they cruised into a 5-2 lead, Liverpool's response coming from Jack Parkinson when the score was 3-1.

Kicking into the Kop in the second half, where most of their supporters were gathered, Parkinson quickly pulled one back for Liverpool then Ronald Orr, a former Newcastle player, struck twice to make it 5-5. The winning goal came five minutes from time from a move that was started by Orr and culminated in Arthur Goddard heading in a John MacDonald cross.

1910
FIRST
FOREIGN TOUR

At the end of the 1909-10 season Liverpool played matches abroad for the first time, when they went on a tour of Denmark and Sweden.

The players set off from Liverpool Central station on 11th May without regular keeper Sam Hardy who had injured his arm. They took a train to Hull then ferry to the Danish capital Copenhagen, with many of the players suffering seasickness during the long crossing.

After a few days in Copenhagen they moved on to the Swedish city of Gothenburg, where they played games against a Stockholm XI and Örgryte, winning 2-0 and 3-0 respectively.

They then returned to Copenhagen where they surprisingly lost 3-0 to a Danish XI in a game that was played in searing heat, but the Reds won the next encounter 1-0 a few days later.

During their trip Liverpool's players met with those of Manchester City, who were touring the same region and were also entertained and taken for trips by their hosts, including to a waterfall and on a tour of Copenhagen's harbour.

They returned to Liverpool by ferry and train, arriving home on 27th May with the *Evening Express* newspaper reporting that they had "evidently thoroughly enjoyed themselves."

1914
FIRST
FA CUP FINAL

Liverpool reached the FA Cup final for the first time in 1914, where they were beaten 1-0 by Burnley in a match that was watched by King George V.

The Reds had a very disappointing league campaign, finishing 16th out of 20 teams, but in the FA Cup they were drawn against lower division opposition in the first four rounds, defeating Barnsley, Gillingham, West Ham United and Queens Park Rangers.

In the semi-final Liverpool were paired with holders Aston Villa who were second in the league, but the Reds caused a shock by beating them 2-0 at White Hart Lane with Jimmy Nicholl scoring both the goals.

The final against Burnley was played at Crystal Palace in London and was watched by 72,778 people. Amongst those present was King George V, the first time a reigning monarch has watched the showpiece event and beforehand the band of the King's Liverpool Regiment played as the National Anthem was sung.

Unfortunately for the Reds they were unable to get their hands on the cup. After an evenly matched first half, Burnley took the lead after 57 minutes, Bert Freeman's first time shot giving keeper Ken Campbell no chance. For a while Burnley threatened to score a second but although the Reds did rally late on and forced three saves from the opposition keeper, no equaliser was forthcoming. Despite losing the final, Liverpool's players were rewarded with another trip to Scandinavia where they played seven matches.

1915
LIVERPOOL FIX MATCH
TO HELP UNITED

One of the most unsavoury moments in Liverpool's history came in 1915. In what would be an unthinkable occurrence nowadays, some Reds players agreed to deliberately lose a match against Manchester United at Old Trafford so they could profit from a betting scam.

With six games remaining Liverpool were comfortably placed in mid-table but United were struggling near the bottom and desperately needed points in the fight against relegation.

United won the game 2-0, a result that bookmakers had been offering odds of 7/1 against. The referee himself noted Liverpool's apparent lack of commitment in the game and the fact that when Fred Pagnam, who wasn't involved in the plot hit the bar late on, some teammates were remonstrating with him.

When it was revealed that several bets had been placed on a 2-0 win for United, an investigation was launched by the FA. Pagnam gave evidence against his teammates and four Liverpool players were banned for life, along with three from United. The Reds players to be banned were Thomas Fairfoul, Tom Miller, Bob Pursell and Jackie Sheldon, with Sheldon, a former United player, having been the ringleader.

With the First World War now raging, football was suspended and the bans lifted in 1919 in recognition of the players service to their country. Three of the banned Liverpool players were forgiven and allowed to play for the club again although Fairfoul, who was 38 by the time organised football resumed, didn't resurrect his career.

Liverpool full back Ephraim Longworth became the first Reds player to captain England in 1921.

Longworth had joined the club from Southern League side Leyton in 1910 and soon became a favourite with the Liverpool crowd but his career was interrupted by the 1st World War.

On 21st May 1921, at the age of 32, he made only his second appearance for England but such was his experience and quality he was chosen to captain the side against Belgium in Brussels, a game England won.

Longworth played three more times for England and appeared a total of 370 times for the Reds, where although not the captain he was a crucial member of the solid defence that helped them to the Football League Championship in 1922 and 1923.

Amazingly he didn't score in any of his Liverpool appearances, the last of which was in 1928 when he was 40 years old. He explained in his *Liverpool Echo* column though that the reason for his lack of goals was because he felt his primary role was to defend and not leave room for the opposing attackers.

After retiring from playing he was given a coaching role at Anfield and died in 1968. In 2002 he was named as one of the two players from the 1920s to be represented in the Liverpool FC Hall of Fame.

Liverpool won the Football League Championship two years running in 1922 and 1923, emulating a feat that had last been achieved by Sheffield Wednesday in 1903 and 1904.

In 1921-22 the Reds clinched the title on Easter Monday with three games to spare, beating deposed champions Burnley 2-1 at Anfield. The team's success was built from the back, with Elisha Scott a rock in goal and the full back pairing of Ephraim Longworth and Donald MacKinlay consistently solid throughout. Just 36 goals were conceded, the best defensive record in the league.

In 1922-23 Liverpool's excellent form continued but there was a sensation in December when despite being top of the table manager David Ashworth left the club to take over at Oldham Athletic, who were second bottom. The move was never fully explained but it had no impact on the Reds, who continued their good form under former player and Director Matt McQueen, who stepped in to fill the role.

Again the Reds defence was the key to the second successive title success, with the 31 goals conceded making them the meanest in the league. The title was wrapped up with a 1-1 draw against Huddersfield at Anfield on 21st April 1923. With only two points awarded for a win they were five points ahead of Sunderland with two games remaining.

The Reds were unable to make it a hat-trick of titles as they finished a disappointing 12th in 1924, a season Huddersfield won the first of what would be three successive successes for them.

1925
FIRST
FOREIGN PLAYER

In 1925 South African Arthur Riley became the first player from outside the British Isles to play for Liverpool. Born in Boksburg which is near Johannesburg, goalkeeper Riley was signed as an understudy to Elisha Scott in August 1925. He had caught the eye of the Liverpool board ten months earlier when he kept goal for a South African XI that beat the Reds 5-2 in a friendly at Anfield.

Riley made his debut away to Tottenham Hotspur on 24th October 1925, a game the Reds lost 3-1 but due to Scott's consistency he would have to wait until early in 1927-28 before being given an extended run in the side and it was not until 1929-30 that he could confidently call himself the Reds first choice keeper. Even then Scott would not give up his place without a fight and reclaimed it from Riley for much of 1931-32.

In the second half of 1932-33 Riley re-established himself as the number one in what was a poor Reds side that flirted with relegation in 1936 and 1937. His last appearance for Liverpool was in a 2-0 defeat by Manchester United at Old Trafford on 6th May 1939 and he never returned to the club after the Second World War.

1928
THE KOP'S
NEW ROOF

Fans turning up at Anfield for the opening day of the 1928-29 season were glad to see that the most popular part of the ground, the 28,000 capacity Spion Kop terrace, had been covered up to protect them from the elements.

The terrace provided spectators with a great view of the game and surrounding area, but it was also exposed to a biting wind. The board realised that only the very fanatical or very poor would pay to stand there in certain conditions. The decision was taken to put a roof over the terrace, as well as replace the old cinder steps with concrete ones.

All of the work was done during the close season and by linking the roof into the Kemlyn Road and Main stands, 1,000 extra seats were also provided. The new Kop was formally unveiled fifteen minutes before kick off by former manager and Chairman John McKenna, who was now President of the Football League.

Liverpool adapted to the new surroundings well, Billy Millar heading in from Dick Edmed's corner in the first minute to give the Reds the lead. Albert Whitehurst made it 2-0 after half an hour and midway through the second half Millar added another.

After the game McKenna was presented with a gold cigar case by the board but he advised them to invest any further monies in a team worthy of the new surroundings, rather than redevelop further sides of the ground. His advice was heeded and the next major development was not until the early 1960s when the Kemlyn Road stand was built.

The Kop went on to become one of, if not the most famous terrace in world football until it was demolished in 1994.

1930
RECORD
HOME DEFEAT

Liverpool's heaviest ever home defeat came on 19th April 1930 when Sunderland came to Anfield and handed out a 6-0 hammering.

One of the most surprising aspects of such a heavy defeat was the fact that Liverpool were 9th in the table before the game and Sunderland 16th.

The game was played on Easter Saturday and one factor in Sunderland's favour was the fact that on the Good Friday, they had been playing relatively close to Liverpool at Bolton Wanderers, whilst the Reds had, had to travel back from the North East where they played Newcastle United.

Despite the travelling involved the result was still a sensational one. 2-0 down at half time, the Reds were completely undone by Sunderland centre forward Bobby Gurney, who remains their record scorer and hit four of his 228 goals for the club in this game.

This was the second time that season that the Anfield crowd had seen a heaviest home defeat, with Manchester City having won 6-1 there in October, breaking the previous record of 5-0 which had been inflicted by Everton in 1914. The only time Liverpool have conceded six goals at Anfield since was in 2007, when Arsenal won 6-3 in a League Cup tie.

1933
THE HIGHEST SCORING
MERSEY DERBY

One of the most entertaining Merseyside derbies was at Anfield on 11th February 1933 when eleven goals were scored as Liverpool won 7-4.

There was not much optimism among Liverpool fans before the game. The Reds hadn't won a derby for six years and Everton were the reigning league champions. To the fans surprise the directors (who picked the team then), picked a youthful side whereas the Everton line-up was packed with experience, including the legendary goalscorer Dixie Dean.

However as derbies so often do, the game went against the form book, with Liverpool overcoming an early goal from Dean to go 3-1 up through Harold Barton, Alf Hanson and Tom Morrison. Although Tommy Johnson pulled one back for Everton just before half time Liverpool regained the advantage after the break as Barton got another and then Harold Taylor made it 5-2 after 68 minutes.

Dean scored his second to give Everton a glimmer of hope with fifteen minutes remaining but within a minute Syd Roberts had restored Liverpool's three goal advantage. Barton completed his hat-trick with five minutes to go to make it 7-3 and there was still time for Jimmy Stein to get Everton's fourth in the 87th minute.

The following Monday the *Daily Post & Mercury's* columnist Stork said he had never seen a more thrilling game and that this derby was 'one of the best, if not the best, of a long series'. It was just a shame that only 44,000, about 75% of the ground's capacity were inside Anfield, due to it being a cold damp day and the Depression meaning fans' money was scarce.

1934
ELISHA SCOTT
LEAVES

At the end of the 1933-34 season legendary Irish goalkeeper Elisha Scott's Liverpool career drew to a close after 22 years with the Reds.

Scott had joined Liverpool in September 1912 after he had been rejected by Everton for being too small. He made his debut at Newcastle on New Year's Day 1913 but didn't establish himself in the side until 1914-15, only for the First World War to put his playing career on hold.

Scott was a key member of the title winning sides of 1922 and 1923, his agility in making saves and brave instinct to dive at forwards feet making up for his lack of height. By the end of the decade he seemed to have lost his place to Arthur Riley but he re-established himself for two seasons between 1931 and 1933. However by the start of 1933-34 he was 40 years old and featured just ten times that season, his last game being a 2-0 defeat at Chelsea on 21st February.

The board's decision to transfer list him in April 1934 angered fans and before the final home game of the season he was allowed to give a farewell address, an unprecedented move. He then returned to his native Ulster to become player manager of Belfast Celtic, continuing to play in goal for another two years. He went on to lead the club to ten Irish League titles and six cups before the club withdrew from the league in 1949 following Sectarian violence at games.

1935
BIGGEST
DERBY WIN

Just three seasons after beating Everton 7-4 in the highest scoring Merseyside derby, Liverpool recorded the biggest margin of victory when they thrashed the Blues 6-0 at Anfield on 7th September 1935.

It was only the third game of the season and Liverpool had lost one and drawn one of their opening two fixtures, while Everton had won one and lost one.

Fred Howe gave Liverpool a fifteenth minute lead when he glanced a header into the goal from Lance Carr's cross. Although Everton threatened to equalise, they were dealt a blow midway through the half when Dixie Dean was forced off with a toe injury. In the 28th minute the Reds took full advantage of this as Gordon Hodgson scored with one of the hardest shots ever seen at Anfield. Although Dean came back onto the field he was ineffective and Hodgson and Lowe each added another to make the score 4-0 at half time.

In the second half Dean was forced to play on despite his injury as substitutes weren't permitted then and Ben Williams was also having a problem with his thigh.

The Reds dominated possession but were unable to convert their chances and were guilty of sloppy passing at times. In the last five minutes though, Howe scored two more, both from headers, to bring his personal total to four and leave the final scoreline as 6-0.

The result has never been bettered in the Merseyside derby and Fred Howe remained the only player to score a derby hat-trick at Anfield until Steven Gerrard in 2011-12.

1937
JOHN MCKENNA
REMEMBERED

When Liverpool played Brentford at Anfield on 27th February 1937 a memorial tablet was unveiled in memory of former manager and Chairman John McKenna, who had died the previous March.

It was Ulsterman McKenna who had been one of the first joint managers of the club and had made the successful application to join the Football League in 1893. After recruiting Tom Watson as manager in 1896 he sat on the board and was Chairman from 1909 to 1914 and 1917 to 1919 before leaving the club in 1921.

McKenna was also very much involved in the administration of the game nationally, becoming President of the Football League in 1910, a position he held until his death at the age of 81. He was also Vice-President of the Football Association from 1928.

The memorial in the Main Stand was unveiled by Everton's Chairman Will Cuff, who was also Vice-President of the Football League and he described McKenna, referred to in football circles as 'Honest John', as a "football genius."

The tablet is still there today but out of sight of the public and Brendan Rodgers, also from Ulster, was photographed standing next to it after he became manager of the club.

BILLY LIDDELL ARRIVES TO DO TWO JOBS

In the summer of 1938 Liverpool signed a sixteen year old prospect called Billy Liddell from Scottish junior club Lochgelly Violet for £175. However Liddell's parents only agreed to his move to England on the basis of the club finding alternative employment for him should his football career not work out.

Mr & Mrs Liddell knew that football was a risky business to get into, especially as the financial rewards for players then were not great and Liddell had looked set to join an accountancy firm in Dunfermline whilst playing part time. When Liverpool expressed an interest, Liddell's parents told officials that they would only agree to their son signing for the club if they could also arrange a job for him.

Liverpool agreed to their request and arranged for Liddell to have a position in a local accountancy firm, as well as lodgings near Anfield where his landlady would be Mrs Doig, widow for the club's former goalkeeper Ned Doig. Liddell would also be paid £1 a week pocket money until he signed professional forms on his seventeenth birthday the following Saturday.

Despite the outbreak of the Second World War delaying his debut by eight years, Liddell went on to become one of Liverpool's greatest ever players, winning the title with them in 1947 and remaining loyal to the club after relegation to the 2nd Division. When he finally retired in 1960 after 22 years with the club he was Liverpool's oldest outfield player, a record later broken by Kenny Dalglish.

Amazingly Liddell achieved everything he did with

the club as a part time player, training just twice a week.

As well as his accountancy job he also found time to be a Magistrate, teach at a local Sunday School and volunteer as a disc jockey at Alder Hey hospital.

1942
BILL SHANKLY
PLAYS FOR LIVERPOOL

Seventeen years before he became manager of Liverpool, Bill Shankly made a guest appearance for the club in a wartime fixture.

During the Second World War most of the players were serving in the armed forces and stationed in various parts of the country. It meant that they and clubs weren't bound by the usual contractual constraints for matches, which were organised on a regional basis.

For a Football League Northern Section match against Everton on 30th May 1942 Shankly, a Scottish international who played for Preston North End but was stationed in Manchester, guested for Liverpool at right half. Shankly was the most high profile of six guest players in the Reds side, another of whom was Burnley's Arthur Woodruff.

In front of a crowd of 13,761, Shankly helped the Reds to a 4-1 win with the goals coming from Len Carney, John Wharton and Cyril Done (2).

During the war Shankly also guested for Arsenal, Luton, Norwich and Partick Thistle and after returning to Preston in 1945 he played for a further four years before moving into management.

1945
MATT BUSBY
27 TURNS DOWN COACHING ROLE

In 1945 former Liverpool player Matt Busby was offered a coaching role at Anfield but chose to take up position of manager at Manchester United instead.

Busby, a half back who had formerly played for Manchester City, joined Liverpool in March 1936 and over the next three seasons helped the club consolidate in mid table after being in danger of relegation. The outbreak of the Second World War cut short his playing career and as vice-captain of the club, he set an example and signed up for service with the King's Liverpool Regiment persuading his teammates to do so as well.

When hostilities ended he signed for Liverpool again and was offered a post as assistant to manager George Kay, but as his views of how football should be played differed with those of the board he turned it down and accepted the vacant manager's job at Manchester United instead.

Although Busby would go on to achieve great success with United, winning five league titles, two FA Cups and a European Cup, he also played his part in the future success of Liverpool. His actions may not have seemed so important at the time but had he not made George Kay aware of Billy Liddell's availability in 1938, or helped a young Bob Paisley to settle in after he arrived from Bishop Auckland a year later, things at Anfield may have turned out very differently.

1946
JACK BALMER'S
TRIPLE HAT-TRICK

On 23rd November 1946 Liverpool forward Jack Balmer completed a remarkable achievement when he hit his third successive hat-trick.

31 year old Balmer had lost the best days of his career to the Second World War and he was never a crowd favourite at Anfield where the regulars preferred Cyril Done and Billy Liddell, often accusing Balmer of shirking tackles.

However even his fiercest critics had to applaud this achievement, which began two weeks earlier when he hit all three goals in a 3-0 win over Portsmouth at Anfield. A week later Liverpool travelled to the East Midlands to face Derby County and in a devastating seventeen minute spell he scored all of the Reds goals in a game they won 4-1.

The stage was then set for Balmer to make history but although he put Liverpool 1-0 up against Arsenal with a fifteenth minute penalty, the Reds were 2-1 behind at half time. However Balmer scored in the 61st and 68th minutes to put Liverpool back in the lead and complete his hat-trick, with Albert Stubbins making it 4-2 in the 78th minute.

The following week Balmer was unable to continue his remarkable run as Liverpool lost 3-2 at Blackpool. A one club player, he retired in 1952 after scoring 110 goals in 309 appearances. The only other players to score three successive hat tricks are Tottenham Hotspur's Frank Osborne in 1925 and Leeds United's Tom Jennings in 1926.

1947
WINNING THE
TITLE IN JUNE

Liverpool won the Football League Championship for the fifth time in 1947, finally being confirmed as champions in the middle of June two weeks after their last league fixture.

Although Liverpool started the season well they were replaced at the top in December by Wolverhampton Wanderers, who beat them 5-1 at Anfield. Wolves seemed unstoppable but wobbled in early May, allowing Liverpool to catch up and the Reds then beat them 2-1 at Molineux on the last day of the month to go top of the table in what was the last game for both teams.

However, one of the coldest winters on record which led to many matches being postponed meant that other teams still had games to play, including Stoke City who would become champions if they won their last match at Sheffield United on 14th June.

On that day Liverpool were playing Everton at Anfield in the Liverpool Senior Cup final, which kicked off fifteen minutes before the Stoke game. Goals from Jack Balmer and William Watkinson put the Reds 2-0 up in the first fifteen minutes and the rest of the game was played at walking pace with the players minds clearly elsewhere.

When it was announced over the loudspeaker that Stoke had lost 2-1 the game came to a standstill as players stopped to shake hands with each other. At the final whistle fans swarmed onto the pitch and hoisted their heroes shoulder high.

The Sheffield United player who had handed Liverpool the title was Jack Pickering, a 40 year old who was making his only appearance of the season.

1948
LIVERPOOL PLAY MANCHESTER UNITED AWAY... IN LIVERPOOL

In 1947-48 Liverpool were drawn to play away to Manchester United in the 4th round of the FA Cup, but the match was actually played half a mile from Anfield at Everton's Goodison Park.

At the time United's Old Trafford ground was out of use after suffering bomb damage during the Second World War and they were playing home games at Manchester City's Maine Road. But with City being drawn at home as well, United had to look for an alternative venue for the tie.

In choosing Goodison they were guaranteed a bumper gate but it was also a gamble, given the majority of the crowd were likely to be backing the Reds. However with United fifth in the league and Liverpool sixteenth they had every reason to believe they could still win the game. In front of a massive crowd of 74,721 Liverpool started the better side and in the first twenty minutes Jack Balmer had a shot cleared off the line and Cyril Done's effort went just wide. However this spurred United into action and they scored three goals in a seven minutes spell between the 30th and 37th minutes.

Only a blatant display of exhibitionism by United in the second half stopped them from doubling the scoreline and the Reds, who had reached the semi-finals of the FA Cup the year before, would have to wait another two years before they finally made it to Wembley.

1950
LIVERPOOL'S FIRST
WEMBLEY VISIT

In 1949-50 Liverpool played at Wembley for the first time but there was disappointment as Arsenal beat them 2-0 in the FA Cup final.

Liverpool reached Wembley by beating Blackburn Rovers, Exeter City, Stockport County, Blackpool and Everton. In the semi-final against Everton at Manchester City's Maine Road, Bob Paisley and Billy Liddell scored the goals on a day many Manchester pubs ran out of beer due to the number of Merseysiders attending the game.

For the final, Liverpool received only 8,000 tickets and received ten times as many applications in a ballot, which was only open to people who lived within 25 miles of the city. The main talking point when the big day arrived was the team selection, with the board opting to drop Bob Paisley and play Bill Jones instead.

The decision to leave Paisley out of the side cost Liverpool dearly, as a vital link between defence and attack was lost. Arsenal took full advantage and gave the Reds no time to settle, taking the lead after seventeen minutes after Alex Forbes went on a run before playing in Reg Lewis who toe poked the ball past Reds keeper Cyril Done.

Early in the second half Jimmy Payne had a great chance to equalise when Billy Liddell crossed for him, but his header was well held on the line by the Arsenal keeper.

Unfortunately Lewis scored Arsenal's second in the 63rd minute, this time hitting a hard low shot past Sidlow after being set up by Freddie Goring-Cox. In a desperate attempt to get back into the game Billy Liddell switched from the left wing into the centre but there was no way back for Liverpool, who had also faced disappointment in the league, finishing eighth after going unbeaten for the first nineteen games.

1951
BILL SHANKLY
TURNS DOWN ANFIELD JOB

The 1950s were not a good decade for Liverpool but things could have been far different had they appointed Bill Shankly in the summer of 1951.

George Kay, who had led Liverpool to the title in 1946 and FA Cup final in 1950 resigned in January 1951 due to ill health, leading to the Reds board inviting applications for the vacant post.

One of them came from Bill Shankly, whose Carlisle United side were pushing for promotion from the 3rd Division North and held Arsenal to a 0-0 draw at Highbury in the 3rd round of the FA Cup, before losing the replay 4-1.

Although the board were interested in appointing Shankly there was a problem from his point of view. That was the fact they selected the team, taking account of the manager's views but making the final decision themselves. Shankly felt this was an unacceptable level of board involvement in team affairs and returned to Carlisle, later saying 'What am I manager of?'

Liverpool instead turned to another 3rd Division North manager Don Welsh, who had led Brighton & Hove Albion from the bottom of the table to the top half and earlier captained Charlton Athletic to FA Cup success in 1947.

Shankly remained at Carlisle for the rest of the season, moving to Grimsby Town in the summer, eventually arriving at Anfield in 1959.

Liverpool's record home attendance of 61,905 squeezed into Anfield for an FA Cup 4th round tie with Wolverhampton Wanderers on 2nd February 1952.

The Reds lay in mid-table at the time and the FA Cup gave fans the only hope of silverware. After seeing off Workington, who were bottom of the 3rd Division North in the 3rd round they were paired with the 1949 cup winners. Wolves were emerging as a strong side under the management of Stan Cullis and had a reputation for breaking from defence to attack quickly.

A large contingent from the Black Country swelled the crowd and the gates were shut at 2pm with 25,000 being on the Kop alone. Liverpool sprung a surprise on the opposition when Billy Liddell was named as centre forward instead of at outside left and amidst the confusion this caused the Wolves defence the Reds were 2-0 up in the first nine minutes through goals from Bob Paisley and Cyril Done.

Although Jimmy Mullen pulled a goal back for Wolves after 72 minutes Liverpool held on for victory. However there was to be no return to Wembley as in the following round they were beaten 2-0 at Burnley.

Ironically, Liverpool provided the opposition for the record crowd at Wolves' Molineux ground. In the 5th round of the FA Cup in 1938-39 61,315 were present for a game that the Reds lost 4-1.

1953
LAST DAY
ESCAPE

On the last day of 1952-53 there was relief for Liverpool and Chelsea after both teams avoided relegation to the 2nd Division following their meeting at Anfield.

Five teams were battling to avoid the remaining relegation place on a dramatic last day of the season. The Reds had slipped towards the danger zone after winning only one of their last nine games and were fourth bottom, knowing a win would ensure they stayed up. If they drew or lost though, they would be sweating on the results of Manchester City and Sheffield Wednesday, both of whom were at home. Sixth bottom Chelsea knew a draw would keep them up, but a defeat could see them relegated and the other team in the mix, Stoke City, needed a draw at home to already relegated Derby County.

A 33rd minute goal from Bill Jones eased Liverpool's nerves and Louis Bimpson made sure of the victory in the 82nd minute to keep the Reds in the top flight. Elsewhere, Manchester City and Sheffield Wednesday won 5-0 and 4-0 respectively to ensure their survival leaving Chelsea nervously awaiting the end of the Stoke v Derby game. To everybody's surprise, Stoke lost 2-1 meaning they were down and Chelsea had survived by the skin of their teeth.

1954
RECORD
DEFEAT

1954 was not a good year for Liverpool fans as relegation was followed by the club's worst ever defeat.

Liverpool never looked like surviving the drop in 1953-54 and were relegated following a 1-0 defeat at home to Cardiff City on Easter Saturday when there were still two more games remaining.

To compound the Reds misery, Everton were promoted to the 1st Division themselves and some crew members working on the liner Queen Mary held a mock funeral service in which a red coffin was lowered into the water.

Liverpool's first season in the 2nd Division for fifty years started badly and fans feared a further relegation to the 3rd Division after just one win in the first eight games. The low point came on 11th December when Birmingham City thrashed them 9-1 at St Andrews.

On a slippery surface, the Reds were one down after just 48 seconds after a deflected goal and it was 3-0 after just fifteen minutes. Although Billy Liddell took advantage of a Birmingham player losing his footing to hit a screamer into the top corner the home side soon added another to make it 4-1 at half time.

Within ten minutes of the restart Liverpool were 6-1 down and had no answer to Birmingham's attacking play, as they hit the bar twice before making it 7-1 in the 77th minute. There was still no let up for the Reds and two goals within a minute of each other six minutes from time completed the rout.

The defeat left the Reds fifteenth in the table and they finished the season in eleventh place, their lowest ever league position. It would be eight long years before they got out of the 2nd Division.

1955
FAN HELPS KNOCK
EVERTON OUT OF THE FA CUP

There was very little to cheer for Liverpool fans in the 2nd Division days but one game to remember was an FA Cup 4th round tie on 29th January 1955 when Everton were beaten 4-0 at Goodison Park, in part thanks to a tip from a fan.

This meeting was the first between the two clubs since 1951 and interest in the game was huge, with over 100,000 applications being received for 72,000 tickets. Only the most optimistic of Reds expected victory though, with Everton riding high in fifth place in the 1st Division, meaning some bookmakers were giving odds of 6/1 against a Reds win.

Billy Liddell gave Liverpool the lead in the eighteenth minute, scoring after controlling a cross, then after half an hour the Reds worked a rehearsed free kick to perfection to go 2-0 up. A fan had written to manager Don Welsh saying that Everton always employed the offside trap at free kicks and the players worked on this in training. As expected, Everton played the offside and Eric Anderson ran with the ball before laying off to Alan A'Court who sprang the trap before firing past Jimmy O'Neill.

Early in the second half defender Laurie Hughes was injured and with no substitutes allowed he was forced to limp along on the wing with Geoff Twentyman dropping into defence. He controlled the threat of Dave Hickson perfectly and in the 57th minute Johnny Evans gave the Blues a mountain to climb when he scored from the rebound after Anderson's shot was parried. Evans completed the rout with fifteen minutes remaining when he headed home a Brian Jackson cross.

Despite this great result the Reds were brought back down to earth in the 5th round going down 2-0 at home to Huddersfield Town.

1956
CUP HEARTBREAK WITH LAST MINUTE DISALLOWED GOAL

Liverpool were cruelly denied extra time in an FA Cup 5th round replay against Manchester City at Anfield on 22nd February 1956 when the referee blew for full time before a shot hit the back of the net.

With Manchester City then a division above Liverpool, the Reds had done well to get a 0-0 draw at Maine Road in the first game. The replay was played on a Wednesday afternoon as there were no floodlights at Anfield then but 57,528 still turned out to see the game.

On a snow covered pitch City had some good chances to go ahead early on but they were wasted by Billy Spurdle and Joe Hayes. The Reds best chance before half time came when Jimmy Payne's cross was blocked on the line by Bill Leivers and bounced off the crossbar.

In the 52nd minute Alan Arnell gave Liverpool the lead after Johnny Evans had hit a long ball into the box but City were level after 64 minutes when Jack Dyson lobbed Reds keeper Dave Underwood. With a minute remaining and the game heading for extra time City went ahead when Bobby Johnstone passed for Hayes who made the score 2-1 to City.

The drama wasn't over though and in injury time Billy Liddell ran from the halfway line, cut inside from the left and hit an unstoppable shot past City keeper Bert Trautmann. As the crowd celebrated, the referee unbelievably ruled the goal out, saying that he had blown the whistle as Liddell was taking his shot. Such was the confusion in the ground that a loudspeaker announcement had to be made stating there would be no extra time and Liverpool had been denied the chance of a home quarter-final tie with Everton.

1957
ANFIELD'S FIRST
FLOODLIGHTS

The first game under floodlights at Anfield took place on 30th October 1957.

Liverpool and Everton both installed their lights at the same time and to celebrate the switch on they played each other in a two legged competition called the Floodlit Challenge Cup. However, they weren't the first floodlights in a football ground in the city, the first club to have them was non-league South Liverpool in 1949.

Unlike the current floodlights which run along the roof of the two stands at the side of the pitch, these lights were installed on four pylons, one in each corner of the ground. Club Chairman T. V. Williams stated that they weren't being installed for financial gain and that the club would be resisting the temptation to play high profile glamour friendlies under the lights, something some other clubs had done.

Instead, he confirmed that the priority was to get Liverpool back into the 1st Division as quickly as possible. The lights had been installed simply so that games didn't come to an end in bad light and that midweek cup replays could be played of an evening rather than in the afternoon.

In the inaugural game, Liverpool beat Everton 3-2 in front of 46,274 fans, meaning that Everton were presented with the trophy having won the first leg 2-0 a fortnight earlier.

1959
NEW STRIKERS AND
A NEW MANAGER JOIN REDS

The latter months of 1959 were quite eventful for Liverpool fans as the club continued to struggle in their quest to get out of the 2nd Division.

Former captain Phil Taylor, who was appointed manager in 1956, was now living on borrowed time following a humiliating FA Cup defeat at non league Worcester City the previous January.

With Billy Liddell's playing days drawing to a close new options up front were needed and Roger Hunt, a youngster signed from Warrington non-league club Stockton Heath, was given a chance against Scunthorpe in September and scored in a 2-1 win.

Two months later, Taylor stunned both Liverpool and Everton fans by signing Everton hero Dave Hickson. Many Reds fans threatened to boycott matches but there were 49,981 inside Anfield for his debut against Aston Villa, in which Hickson scored both goals in a 2-1 win.

The following week Hickson and Hunt were both on the scoresheet in a 4-2 defeat at Lincoln City, but although they were delivering the rest of the team weren't. The result left the Reds eleventh in the table and this game, played on 14th November, turned out to be Taylor's last match in charge.

In the middle of December Liverpool appointed Bill Shankly as manager, the Scot having agreed to leave Huddersfield Town to join the Reds. Things at Anfield would never be the same again.

1960
BILL SHANKLY
FACES HIS BROTHER

Bill Shankly was not the only footballing person in his family, in fact all four of his brothers played professionally with one of them also becoming a successful manager.

In March 1960, three months after joining the Reds, Bill took his Liverpool team to Scotland to face older brother Bob's Dundee side in a friendly at Dens Park, arranged to celebrate the switch on of the home club's new floodlights.

In front of a crowd of 12,000 on a bitterly cold night, there was little action on the pitch to warm the crowd up and the match was very much played on an exhibition basis with not much goalmouth incident in the first half.

At half time members of the Hawkhill Harriers organised some races around the running track that surrounded the pitch, with the seniors racing for a mile and the juniors doing two laps (about half a mile).

The only goal of the game came in the second half after Reds keeper Bert Slater misjudged a corner kick and although he caught the ball, stepped back with it over the line. Roger Hunt missed a good chance to draw Liverpool level late on in the game meaning it was Bob of the two Shankly brothers who ended up coming out on top.

Like Bill, Bob would go on to enjoy managerial success himself, winning the Scottish League Championship in 1962 and reaching the semi-finals of the European Cup the following year.

1961
THE SAINT
BECOMES A SINNER

FACT 41

In May 1961 Liverpool's record signing had an eventful start to his career, hitting a hat-trick and then getting sent off in his first few games.

Liverpool paid £37,500, twice as much as they had ever spent on any player before, for Motherwell's Scottish international Ian St John. Although he signed too late to play in Liverpool's last game of 1960-61 against Stoke City, St John was available for the Liverpool Senior Cup final against Everton at Goodison Park a week later.

St John made his own way to Goodison by bus and at first stewards at the players' entrance refused to believe he was part of the Liverpool team. Perhaps they should have continued to refuse entry, as St John went on to score a hat-trick in the match, which was the main talking point of it despite Everton's 4-3 win.

The next week Liverpool went on tour to Czechoslovakia where they played four games. After scoring in the first game which the Reds drew 2-2 with

Jihonaravsky Kraj, St John again made all the headlines in the third game against Tatran Presov. Although he scored Liverpool's goal in a 1-1 draw, he was sent off fifteen minutes from time for retaliation after being kicked by a Presov player.

St John was so upset at the nature of his dismissal that he wrote a lengthy piece for the *Daily Post* regarding the incident, in which he maintained he was angry at not having been awarded a penalty a minute earlier and then had been kicked twice and although he raised his foot, he withdrew it and didn't connect with anybody.

Later that summer St John's compatriot Ron Yeats arrived from Dundee United and together they would play a massive part in Liverpool's success over the next decade.

1962
LIV-ER-POOL
'CLAP CLAP CLAP'

In 1961-62 Liverpool finally won promotion to the 1st Division after eight seasons of trying, leading to wild celebrations at the end.

The Reds won ten out of their first eleven games and never looked like missing out on promotion. The game at which it could all be wrapped up was on Easter Saturday, 21st April 1962, when Southampton came to Anfield.

On a rain sodden day, Ian St John was suspended but his replacement Kevin Lewis scored twice in the first half hour to ease the nerves of any Kopites who felt they may be on the brink of blowing their chances again.

Southampton rarely threatened and even though the pitch was a quagmire the Reds created more chances with Roger Hunt and Gerry Byrne going close, then Lewis almost got his hat-trick but he couldn't connect with an Ian Callaghan cross.

The final whistle meant that Liverpool had secured promotion with five games left and there were wild celebrations at the end as the players went on a lap of honour and many fans poured onto the pitch.

After the players went off down the tunnel they re-appeared in the directors' box after calls from the crowd for them to return. Both players and fans then engaged in the rhythmic chant of 'Liv-er-pool clap clap clap', a chant that is still often heard at Liverpool matches today.

1963
LAST MINUTE PENALTY SETTLES
MUCH POSTPONED CUP TIE

The harsh winter of 1963 played havoc with the fixture list, with Liverpool's FA Cup 4th round replay against Burnley finally being settled nearly a month after the first game thanks to a last minute penalty by Ronnie Moran.

The two sides drew 1-1 at Turf Moor on 26th January but with the whole of Britain shivering in Arctic conditions, the replay was postponed several times and the Anfield pitch wasn't playable again until 20th February, after the 5th round ties were meant to have taken place.

In front of 57,906 fans, a crowd that has never been equalled at Anfield since, Alex Elder gave the visitors the lead in the 24th minute but on the stroke of half time Ian St John equalised.

With a second replay looming the Reds were awarded a penalty in the last minute of extra time when St John blocked a clearance by Burnley keeper Adam Blacklaw and as the ball bounced towards goal, Blacklaw bundled St John over as he ran to help it on its way into an empty net.

The referee awarded a penalty but Blacklaw escaped with only a booking. With the crowd deathly silent Ronnie Moran stepped forward to take the penalty and hit it powerfully to Blacklaw's right as he dived to his left. The celebrations had hardly stopped when the full time whistle was blown, meaning Liverpool would now have a trip to Highbury to face Arsenal in the next round.

Despite their heroic efforts, which saw Liverpool make it all the way to the semi-final, they were denied a trip to the final by Leicester City, who beat them 1-0 in a game in which their keeper Gordon Banks was outstanding.

1964
THE PAPIER MÂCHÉ
TITLE TROPHY

Just two years after being promoted from the 2nd Division Liverpool won the Football League championship but their lap of honour saw them carrying a craft version of the trophy.

The Reds had began the season slowly, losing their first three home games and although they went top after a 1-0 win against Manchester United at Old Trafford in November, it was so tight up there that three weeks later they fell to fourth after a home defeat to Blackburn Rovers.

Liverpool hit the top again on Easter Monday when they beat fellow title chasers Tottenham Hotspur 3-1 at Anfield, one of three wins in four days over the holiday period. Further wins over Manchester United and Burnley meant victory over Arsenal in their final home game would seal the title with three away games still to play.

There was an early scare when Arsenal were awarded a penalty but this was saved by Tommy Lawrence and from then on the result was never in doubt, with the Reds leading 5-0 after an hour. Cameras from the *BBC's Panorama* programme were present to film the crowd, as singing at matches then was a new phenomenon and they put on an excellent show.

When the game ended the only problem was that the Football League had refused to allow the championship trophy to be handed over before the end of the season, even though deposed champions Everton had offered to give it back early. Luckily for the players, a fan had brought along a papier mâché trophy which was paraded by them on their lap of honour.

INTO EUROPE AND AN ALL RED STRIP

FACT 45

After winning the Football League Championship Liverpool entered European competition for the first time in 1964-65 with Bill Shankly deciding an all red strip would be beneficial to them.

The first European tie saw the Reds comfortably beat Icelandic champions KR Reykjavik 11-1 on aggregate, but they were handed a difficult 2nd round encounter when they were paired with Belgian champions Anderlecht. They had provided many of the Belgium side that had been impressive in a 2-2 draw with England a month before the 1st leg.

A few days before the game Shankly asked captain Ron Yeats to try on a pair of red shorts as he believed they would have a psychological impact and make the players look bigger and more intimidating. After looking Yeats up and down Shankly then stood on the pitch and saw him walk out of the tunnel, concluding that he looked about seven feet tall. At the suggestion of Ian St John, it was decided to go the whole hog and wear red socks as well.

After Liverpool won the game 3-0 that was it, the all red strip was well and truly here to stay after 68 years of playing in white shorts and socks. Although Liverpool got past Anderlecht there would be no European glory that season as they were beaten by Inter Milan in the semi-finals.

1965
EE AYE ADDIO
THE QUEEN'S WEARING RED

FACT **46**

When Liverpool finally won the FA Cup in 1965 even the Queen appeared to be on the Reds side. The club hadn't had much luck in the FA Cup in their 73 year history, losing two finals and five semi-finals. A poor start to the 1964-65 league season, with five of the first eight games lost meant retaining the title was never a realistic possibility and Bill Shankly made it a top priority to win the FA Cup.

Shankly believed that it was a disgrace that a club of Liverpool's size had never won the FA Cup and that the fans had to put up with the taunts of other supporters regarding this. It was even suggested by Evertonians that if Liverpool did ever win the cup the Liver Birds would fly away from their perch atop the Liver Buildings.

Liverpool beat West Bromwich Albion, Stockport County, Bolton Wanderers and Leicester City to reach the semi-finals, where they beat Chelsea 2-1 at Villa Park. In the final they would face an emerging Leeds United side, who had only been promoted the previous season but finished second in the league.

Defender Gerry Byrne broke his collar bone early on but in a remarkable act of bravery he continued playing as there were no substitutes. After ninety minutes the score was 0-0. Three minutes into extra time Roger Hunt headed Liverpool into the lead. Although Billy Bremner equalised, Ian St John headed the winner nine minutes from time to finally end the Reds cup hoodoo.

As Ron Yeats collected the cup from the Queen, Liverpool fans noticed she was wearing a red jacket and quickly sang "Ee aye addio The Queen's wearing red." Whether that is a factor of her not attending a final since isn't clear.

WINNING THE TITLE
WITH FOURTEEN PLAYERS

Given the squad rotation that is common today, it is almost unthinkable that Liverpool won the 1965-66 League Championship using only fourteen players.

Consistency and continuity were the key to Liverpool's title success as no major signings were made and Bill Shankly stuck with the players that had won the FA Cup the previous season.

Of the fourteen players used, two played only six games between them. Shankly would tell the press it was be the 'same team as last year' and it reeled off the tongues easily – Tommy Lawrence, Chris Lawler, Gerry Byrne, Tommy Smith, Ron Yeats, Willie Stevenson, Ian Callaghan, Ian St John, Roger Hunt, Gordon Milne, Peter Thompson. Whenever a player was injured, utility player Geoff Strong would step in to play in their position and he featured 22 times.

The title was confirmed in the penultimate game, a 2-1 win at Anfield over a Chelsea side whose players formed a guard of honour as the Reds players took to the pitch. Despite Chelsea's pleasantries they didn't give the Reds the title on a plate and defended solidly whilst also posing some problems in attack. Liverpool eventually found a breakthrough on 48 minutes when Roger Hunt's shot was deflected into the net by John Dunn. Bert Murray equalised in the 62nd minute only for Hunt to restore the Reds lead seven minutes later and it finished 2-1.

Like two years earlier, the trophy wasn't available to present but the club still had the papier mâché version for the players to parade around the ground as they celebrated a second title success in three years.

1967
KEEPER'S
CARELESS HANDS

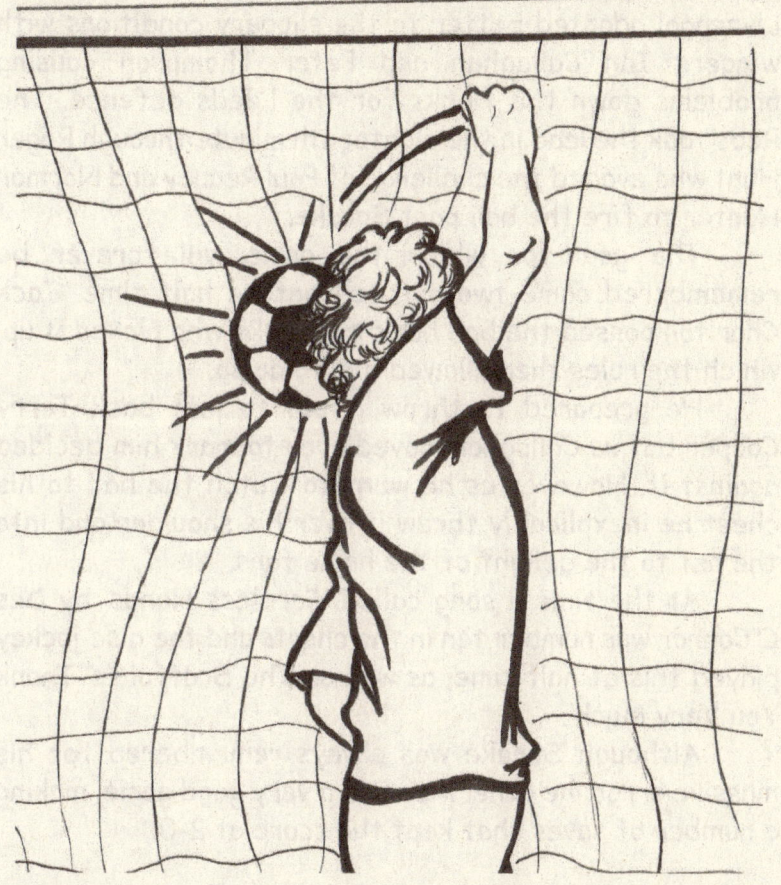

When Liverpool beat Leeds United 2-0 on 9th December 1967 they were given a helping hand for the first goal by opposition keeper Gary Sprake.

Both sides were in contention for the league title along with the two Manchester clubs, with Liverpool lying in second place and Leeds in fourth. Although they had met in the FA Cup final two years earlier, the big rivalry between the two clubs was still a couple of seasons away and the crowd of 39,675 was the lowest of the Reds ten home league games so far.

The pitch was covered in an inch of snow and Liverpool adapted better to the slippery conditions with wingers Ian Callaghan and Peter Thompson causing problems down the flanks for the Leeds defence. The Reds took the lead in the eighteenth minute through Roger Hunt who evaded the challenge of Paul Reaney and Norman Hunter to fire the ball past Sprake.

The goal for which the game will forever be remembered came two minutes before half time. Jack Charlton passed the ball back to Sprake who picked it up, which the rules then allowed him to do so.

He prepared to throw it out to left back Terry Cooper but as Callaghan moved over to mark him decided against it. However as he went to clutch the ball to his chest he inexplicably threw it over his shoulder and into the net to the delight of the home fans.

At the time a song called 'Careless Hands' by Des O'Connor was number ten in the charts and the disc jockey played this at half time, as well as The Scaffold's 'Thank You Very Much'.

Although Sprake was always remembered for his massive error, he otherwise had a very good game, making a number of saves that kept the score at 2-0.

1968
CUP WIN
IN THE FOG

When Liverpool beat Walsall 5-2 in an FA Cup 4th round replay on 19th February 1968 Tony Hateley scored four of Liverpool's goals although due to the fog hardly anybody

can claim to have seen all of them.

The game was played on a Monday night, only two days after the sides had drawn 0-0 at Walsall's Fellows Park ground and another unusual feature was that Liverpool didn't issue a full match programme, instead just producing a single sheet with the team line-ups on it.

The fog was so thick that night that many Liverpool Corporation buses weren't running. This kept the crowd down to 39,113, well below the 54,075 that had watched a 3rd round replay with Bournemouth & Boscombe Athletic.

The Reds kicked into the Kop for the first half and were 3-0 up at half time with Hateley getting two goals and Geoff Strong the other. Fans in the Anfield Road end had no idea what was going on and only knew the score and scorers due to the three roars which were followed by the singing of the players' names.

In the second half, Hateley completed his hat-trick after 64 minutes and whilst the roar was not so great, the Kop knew there had been a goal. They sang 'We want to know who scored' and after the Anfield Road fans replied 'Tony Hateley' the Kop responded by singing 'Thank you very much for Tony Hateley'. The same thing happened after 71 minutes when Hateley got his fourth.

The only goals the Kop saw in that second half were in the last fifteen minutes when Tommy Watson scored twice for Walsall before the majority of fans faced a long walk home in the fog.

1969
LIVERPOOL APPEAR IN FIRST COLOUR MATCH OF THE DAY

In the 1960s football on television was still very much in its early days. The first *Match of the Day* was aired on *BBC2* on the opening day of 1964-65 and featured highlights of Liverpool versus Arsenal but fans would have to wait until 15th November 1969 before they could see their heroes in red.

The *BBC* also chose a Liverpool match for the first colour *Match of the Day*, which was by now broadcasting on *BBC1*. The game against West Ham United appeared a strange choice by the *BBC*, given it was also the Manchester derby that day.

However the programme's producer Alex Weeks felt that for the first colour transmission Anfield was the best setting, given the entertainment provided by both the crowd and players. West Ham's side included England's 1966 World Cup winning captain Bobby Moore and hat trick hero Geoff Hurst, as well as Harry Redknapp and Frank Lampard's father who was also called Frank.

Liverpool won the game 2-0 with the goals coming from Chris Lawler and Bobby Graham and that night the highlights were watched by 10 million people.

Three weeks later Liverpool featured in colour again when the Merseyside derby from Goodison Park was shown, with Liverpool winning 3-0 in a game made most famous for Sandy Brown's headed own goal.

1970
FORMER WELDER
STARTS A REVOLUTION

Liverpool fans have a former welder and pub striker to thank for scoring a shock goal against them that led to Bill Shankly breaking up his first great side.

After finishing second to Leeds United the year before with a points total that was usually enough to win the league, the Reds were very inconsistent in 1969-70. For example, a memorable 3-0 win against leaders Everton was followed by a 4-1 home defeat to Manchester United.

However as long as progress was made in the FA Cup fans were content and Liverpool overcame Coventry City, Wrexham and Leicester City to reach the quarter-finals, where they were handed a relatively straight forward tie away to 2nd Division Watford.

In front of 34,047 fans at Vicarage Road, Liverpool were stunned by 63rd minute header from Barry Endean, a 23 year old former welder who had signed for Watford after being spotted playing parks football in the North East two years earlier.

The following week Bill Shankly wielded the axe for the league trip to Derby County, dropping long standing keeper Tommy Lawrence as well as Ron Yeats and Ian St John, who had been mainstays of the side since the 1961-62 promotion season. For the rest of 1969-70 Shankly continued with experimental line-ups as players who had been learning their trade in the reserves such as Ray Clemence, Larry Lloyd and Alec Lindsay were introduced to the side.

In the semi-final Watford were beaten 5-1 by Chelsea while Endean played the rest of his career in the lower divisions with Charlton Athletic, Blackburn Rovers, Workington, Huddersfield Town and Hartlepool United.

1971
BIG BAMBER AND LITTLE BAMBER

In 1970-71 Bill Shankly continued to create a new look Liverpool side mixing experience with promising youngsters and players who had been plucked from the lower divisions. Two new members were university graduates Steve Heighway and Brian Hall, dubbed 'Big Bamber' and 'Little Bamber' by fans.

Heighway was studying economics at Warwick University when he was spotted playing for Cheshire League side Skelmersdale United in 1970 and Brian Hall first registered as an amateur in 1966 whilst completing his maths studies at Liverpool University.

Winger Heighway put off his plans to become a teacher and signed a one year contract with Liverpool in the summer of 1970 and was soon terrorising full backs. Hall, who had patiently awaited his chance in the reserves, finally established himself in 1970-71 after Ian Callaghan was injured.

Fans nicknamed Heighway 'Big Bamber' and Hall 'Little Bamber' after Bamber Gascoigne, presenter of the television quiz show *University Challenge*.

Both players made their mark in the FA Cup, with Hall scoring his first goal for the club in a 2-1 semi-final win over Everton at Old Trafford. Heighway was on target in the quarter-final, scoring the only goal in a replay against Tottenham Hotspur at White Hart Lane and then the opening goal of the final against Arsenal.

Despite Heighway's goal, the Reds lost the final 2-1 but they were still given a magnificent reception the following day, causing Bill Shankly to ask Hall who the Chinese leader was. After Hall answered 'Chairman Mao' the boss told the crowd 'it's questionable if Chairman Mao of China could have arranged such a show of strength as you have shown yesterday and today.'

1972
21 SUCCESSIVE HOME
LEAGUE WINS

In 1972 Liverpool set a top flight record of 21 consecutive home league wins, a record still standing today.

Nobody could have guessed what was being embarked upon when the Reds beat Crystal Palace 4-1 at Anfield on 29th January, a win that kept them in tenth place in the table. However it was the start of a run of thirteen wins in fourteen games that took the Reds into second place and on the brink of the title. With one hand on the trophy though, it slipped away in the last two games, which were lost 1-0 at eventual champions Derby County and drawn 0-0 with Arsenal.

The home winning run continued into the 1972-73 season, when the Reds won their first twelve home league games, taking the total in succession to 21 as they topped the table. The sequence was eventually broken by Derby County on 20th January 1973 when they snatched a 1-1 draw at a snowy Anfield, making them the first side to leave with any points since Leeds United won 2-0 on New Year's Day the year before.

In March 2012 Manchester City looked set to equal Liverpool's record, only to surprisingly draw 3-3 with Sunderland at the Etihad Stadium. The record number of successive home wins across all four divisions is Bradford Park Avenue's 25, set in the 3rd Division North from 1926 to 1927.

1973
LIVERPOOL NOSE IN FRONT ON GRAND NATIONAL DAY

FACT 54

After seven years without a trophy, Liverpool finally tasted success again with the 1973 League Championship with results on Grand National day going a long way to deciding things.

On 31st March the Reds were at home to Tottenham Hotspur whilst closest rivals Arsenal, who had played a game more, were at home to Derby County. As the Grand National was taking place at Aintree, Liverpool's game kicked off at 11.30am to allow fans to watch the match and race. Such kick offs were rare at the time when it was customary for all fixtures to begin at 3pm on a Saturday.

A win over Tottenham would take them two points clear of Arsenal and really increase the pressure on the Gunners. However a magnificent performance by Spurs keeper Pat Jennings denied the Reds victory.

After going behind against the run of play on 21 minutes the Reds continued to dominate and were awarded a penalty after 39 minutes when Peter Cormack was fouled. Kevin Keegan took the kick but Jennings pushed it away. The equaliser eventually came after 70 minutes when Jennings, who had made several great saves, was deceived by Keegan's mis-hit shot.

Liverpool were awarded another penalty with five minutes to go after a handball on the line. This time Tommy Smith took the kick but again Jennings saved it, leading to the Reds captain sinking to his knees and beating the turf in frustration.

Although the draw was disappointing there was good news later in the day when Arsenal were beaten 1-0 by Derby, and the Reds had edged a little further in front. They secured the title the following month, as well as winning the UEFA Cup.

NINE PLAYERS
ON THE SCORESHEET

FACT 55

When Liverpool recorded their record victory against Norwegian side Strømsgodset in the European Cup Winners Cup in 1974-75 goalkeeper Ray Clemence and midfielder Brian Hall were the only two players not to score.

The Reds had beaten Newcastle 3-0 in the FA Cup final the previous season to qualify for the Cup Winners Cup, but manager Bill Shankly then stunned the club by resigning in the summer. His assistant Bob Paisley was appointed and although he couldn't deliver any trophies in his first season, finishing second in the league, the club did achieve a record victory.

It took the Reds just three minutes to open the scoring against the Norwegian side, when Alec Lindsay converted a penalty and by half time it was 5-0 thanks to two goals from Phil Boersma and one each from Phil Thompson and Steve Heighway.

In the second half it took twenty minutes for Liverpool to add a sixth, which eventually came from Peter Cormack. Thompson then got his second in the 74th minute and two minutes later Emlyn Hughes made it 8-0. Three goals in the last five minutes from Tommy Smith, Ian Callaghan and Steve Heighway completed Strømsgodset's humiliation. It left Hall as the only outfield player not to score.

For the second leg in Oslo which Liverpool won 1-0 Paisley had taken no chances and made only two changes to the side. One of those was forced upon him to an injury to Phil Thompson who was replaced by veteran Chris Lawler and the other saw the club's record signing Ray Kennedy come into the side in place of Peter Cormack.

1976
THE FIRST ENGLISH CLUB
TO WIN AT NOU CAMP

In 1975-76 Liverpool won the UEFA Cup for the second time, beating Bruges 4-3 on aggregate in the final after they had got there with a famous win over Barcelona in the semis.

When the Reds faced Barcelona in the Nou Camp, they were greeted by a chorus of boos from the crowd for wearing an all white strip, the same as their hated rivals Real Madrid. The crowd was soon silenced though when John Toshack calmly chested down a Kevin Keegan pass to hit a shot past Pedro Mora.

Such was Liverpool's dominance in the game that they could have won by four or five goals. In the second half the home fans were so infuriated with their team's inability to threaten the Reds goal that they started to throw cushions towards the pitch. Joey Jones, who was sat on the Reds bench was unaware that this was a demonstration against their own team and threw them back, thinking they'd been aimed at him. He only stopped when Bob Paisley told him there'd be a riot if he carried on.

The win in the Nou camp had been the first time an English club had beaten Barcelona there and Liverpool drew the second leg 1-1 at Anfield to progress to the final. Amazingly in 25 matches against English sides since then up until the end of 2011-12, Barcelona have lost only one, also against Liverpool in 2006-07 when the Reds won 2-1 thanks to goals from Craig Bellamy and John Arne Risse.

A DRAW TO WIN THE LEAGUE, PROVIDING IT'S NOT 3-3

FACT **57**

Bob Paisley won his first title in 1975-76, clinching it in the last game of the season against Wolverhampton Wanderers at Molineux.

This was the last season in which goal average, which was worked out by dividing the number of goals scored by those conceded, was used to separate teams level on points. Going into this game the Reds trailed Queens Park Rangers, who had completed their fixtures, by one point. A win would guarantee the title but the goal average was so tight that if the game was a draw, it had to be 2-2 or below, otherwise QPR would be champions.

To make things more complicated Wolves needed a win to stand any chance of avoiding relegation so there was no chance of an easy ride for Liverpool, who went behind after thirteen minutes to a Steve Kindon goal.

In the second half Liverpool were kicking into the end where an estimated 20,000 of their fans were gathered but even when 'super sub' David Fairclough was sent on after an hour they still couldn't find a breakthrough. Eventually in the 76th minute Kevin Keegan equalised to level the scores and send the visiting fans into raptures and two goals in the last five minutes from John Toshack and Ray Kennedy put the result beyond doubt.

With Birmingham drawing at Sheffield United, meaning Wolves couldn't stay up even if they won there was no danger of a late fightback and the nightmare scenario of a 3-3 draw which would have denied the Reds the title. On the way home there were so many fans on the M6 that traffic ground to a standstill with many getting out of their cars to celebrate on the motorway.

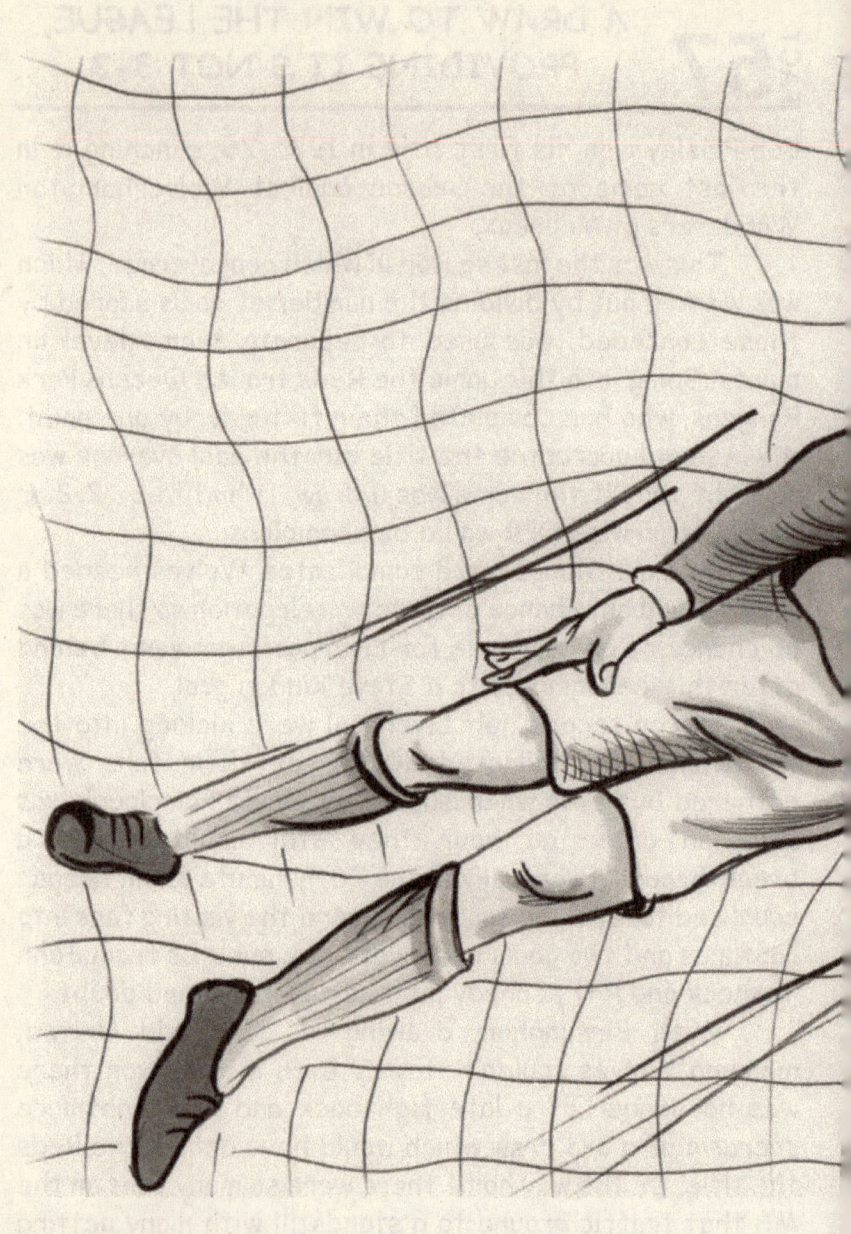

1977
REPLAY DATE WRECKS REDS TREBLE DREAM

The 1976-77 season will forever be remembered for the first European Cup triumph, beating Borussia Mönchengladbach 3-1 in Rome. However the Reds were denied a treble when Bob Paisley tinkered with his team on hearing the FA's plans for a drawn game.

Liverpool clinched the League Championship with a 0-0 draw against West Ham United at Anfield on 14th May but as they prepared for the FA Cup final against Manchester United a week later the FA dropped a bombshell. They announced that any replay would take place on 27th June, claiming that no earlier dates were available due to the Home International Championships and an England tour of South America.

Despite Liverpool's calls for the final to be settled on the day, by penalties if necessary, the FA refused to consider any alternative. Fearful that a draw would disrupt the players' summer rest, Paisley opted for a more attacking side, dropping midfielder Ian Callaghan in favour of David Johnson. The change didn't pay off. An off form Johnson was taken off after an hour with Liverpool trailing 2-1 and Callaghan's introduction failed to change the game.

The disappointment was forgotten though the following Wednesday when over 25,000 Reds fans travelled to Rome for the European Cup Final, seeing their team triumph 3-1 thanks to goals from Terry McDermott, Tommy Smith and Phil Neal. It was Liverpool's third European trophy but the one they craved most. They became only the second English team to win the European Cup and the first to do so on foreign soil. Callaghan was reinstated to the side for the game, making him the only player to appear for the Reds in the 2nd Division and the European Cup final.

1978
THE FIRST
PROFESSIONAL FOUL

The term professional foul was coined after the 1978 League Cup final when Phil Thompson admitted to deliberately fouling an opposition player to prevent him from scoring a goal.

This was Liverpool's first League Cup final and after drawing 0-0 with Nottingham Forest at Wembley on 18th March, a game in which Forest's stand in keeper Chris Woods was outstanding, the two teams met again at Old Trafford four days later.

Forest won the game in controversial fashion after being awarded a penalty in the 53rd minute for a foul by Thompson on John O'Hare, even though television replays showed that the incident had taken place outside the area.

John Robertson converted the kick and Liverpool dominated the game, being infuriated by the referee again when Terry McDermott appeared to have scored an equaliser only to have it ruled out for having controlled the ball with his arm.

To compound the Reds frustration Ian Callaghan was booked for the only time in over 800 appearances for Liverpool and after the match a furious Tommy Smith told reporters that the referee should be shot.

Thompson was quick to admit that he had deliberately brought down O'Hare, knowing that he was outside the area and that bringing somebody down in such circumstances wasn't a red card offence then. However he was soon in hot water with the FA who charged him with bringing the game into disrepute and fined him £300.

1978
HAMMER KEEPS
TOMMY SMITH OUT OF FINAL

FACT 60

When Liverpool beat Bruges 1-0 at Wembley to win their second European Cup they did so without Tommy Smith who had been the hero in Rome a year earlier. The defender who had scored the crucial second goal against Borussia Mönchengladbach was ruled out of the final following a freak injury sustained at home.

Smith played in all six of the matches, against Dynamo Dresden, Benfica and Borussia Mönchengladbach that took Liverpool to the final. However two weeks before the match he was doing some work in his garden at home when a hammer fell on his foot, breaking his toe.

Smith's place was taken by Alan Hansen, who had signed from Partick Thistle a year earlier. On the whole he had little to do against a Bruges side that rarely ventured out of their own half, although he was mightily relieved on 80 minutes when he mis-hit a backpass which was cleared off the line by Phil Thompson.

The only goal of a dour match was settled in the 65th minute when Kenny Dalglish cleverly chipped the keeper after receiving a pass from Graeme Souness.

Liverpool's victory meant they became the first English team to retain the European Cup and it was their third European triumph in succession, having won the UEFA Cup in 1976. However their hopes of a hat-trick of successes were thwarted by Nottingham Forest, who beat the Reds 2-0 on aggregate in the 1st round of the following season's competition.

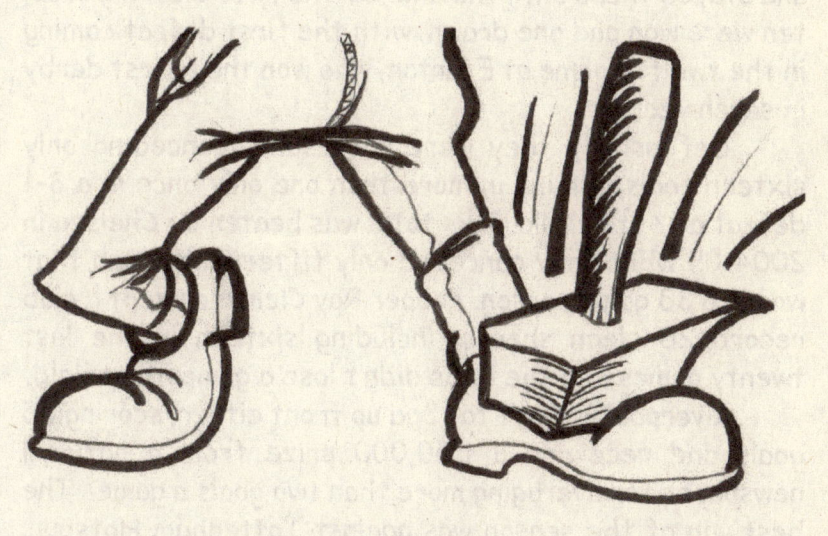

1979
A SEASON
OF SUPERLATIVES

Liverpool's eleventh Football League Championship in 1978-79 set a number of records.

The Reds amassed 68 points, a new record under the two points a win system in a 42 game season. They went top of the league on the second Saturday of the season and stayed there until the end. Of the first eleven games, ten were won and one drawn, with the first defeat coming in the twelfth game at Everton, who won their first derby in seven years.

Defensively they were rock solid, conceding only sixteen goals, letting in more than one only once in a 3-1 defeat at Aston Villa. This total was beaten by Chelsea in 2004-05 when they conceded only fifteen, although that was in a 38 game season. Keeper Ray Clemence kept a club record 28 clean sheets, including sixteen in the last twenty games and the Reds didn't lose a game at Anfield.

Liverpool weren't too bad up front either, scoring 85 goals and receiving a £50,000 prize from a national newspaper for averaging more than two goals a game. The best win of the season was against Tottenham Hotspur, who lost 7-0 at Anfield despite containing two members of the Argentine World Cup winning squad in their side.

A 3-0 home win over Aston Villa with two more away games remaining sealed the title for the Reds, a game that marked the 40th anniversary of manager Bob Paisley first joining the club as a player.

1980

AVI SCORES AT EACH END AS REDS BEAT VILLA FOR TITLE

For the second year running Liverpool clinched the Football League Championship with a win against Aston Villa in their final home game of the season when Israeli defender Avi Cohen scored for both teams.

The Reds weren't as all conquering as the previous season, starting slowly with just two wins in the first seven games. But a 4-0 win at Manchester City on 27th October 1979 set them on a sequence of ten wins from eleven games and after going top on 8th December with a 3-1 win at Aston Villa they were never off it.

For the second season running, Liverpool knew a win in their last home game against Villa would clinch the title. On a sunny Saturday afternoon the Reds got off to a perfect start when David Johnson scored after three minutes, but Cohen sliced a clearance into the roof of his own net midway through the first half.

Five minutes into the second half Cohen made amends for his own goal when he made it 2-1 with a low drive and Johnson got his second after 72 minutes to make the result beyond doubt. An own goal from Noel Blake six minutes later made it 4-1.

Cohen's goal was his only one for the Reds in a two year period that saw him play 24 games. After later playing for Maccabi Tel Aviv and Rangers he died aged just 56 in a motorbike accident in December 2010.

FACT 63
RUN OF 85 HOMES GAMES
UNBEATEN COMES TO AN END

On 31st January 1981 Liverpool's unbeaten home record stretching back three years came to an end in the most surprising of circumstances.

The Reds last home defeat had been on 21st January 1978 when Trevor Francis scored as Birmingham City won 3-2 at Anfield. Over the next three years they went on the unbeaten run that encompassed 63 league and 22 cup games, scoring 212 goals and conceding just 35.

Although they had won the title in 1979 and 1980 Liverpool were not so dominant in 1980-81 and before this match were third in the table, two points behind leaders Aston Villa. However visitors Leicester City were bottom and had won just two of their thirteen games so far so few would have predicted what went on to happen.

Things were going as expected at half time when the Reds led thanks to an own goal from Alan Young, but after the break Leicester came back to win thanks to goals from Pat Byrne and Jim Melrose. It completed a miserable week as Liverpool had been knocked out of the FA Cup by Everton the previous Saturday.

The Reds record has never been equalled by an English club. Although Chelsea went on an 86 home match unbeaten league run between 2004 and 2008, a sequence ended by Liverpool winning 1-0 at Stamford Bridge, they did lose cup games during that time.

1981
LIVERPOOL'S FIRST
SUBSTITUTED SUBSTITUTE

FACT 64

In 1980-81 Liverpool had a disappointing league campaign finishing fifth, but they made up for it with cup success, winning their first League Cup and beating Real Madrid in Paris to become European champions for the third time.

The Reds had reached the final by overcoming all the odds to beat Bayern Munich in the semi-final. After a 0-0 draw at Anfield in the first leg, Liverpool's task in the away leg was made harder by the fact that captain Phil Thompson and left back Alan Kennedy were both ruled out through injury.

The German side were so sure of success that they published a route to Paris and left it on every seat in the stadium prior to the game at their Olympic Stadium, something that riled the Reds players. However after just seven minutes Kenny Dalglish was forced off through injury and replaced by youngster Howard Gayle, playing only his second game for the club. His appearance was so unexpected that the Bayern scouts hadn't even prepared any reports on him and as such he was an unknown quantity, running the home defenders ragged.

Bayern found the only way to deal with Gayle was to foul him and as he began to retaliate he was taken off with twenty minutes to go to ensure he wasn't red carded. With seven minutes remaining in the match Ray Kennedy put the Reds 1-0 up and although Karl Heinz Rummenigge equalised with three minutes left it wasn't enough for the home side and the Reds went through on away goals rule.

In the final in Paris Gayle had to settle for a place on the bench as a goal from Alan Kennedy was enough to secure a third European Cup for Liverpool.

1982
LIVERPOOL GIVE TOTTENHAM FIRST WEMBLEY FINAL DEFEAT

When Liverpool won the League Cup in 1981-82 they became the first side to beat Tottenham Hotspur in a Wembley final. Spurs had won their four Wembley FA Cup and two League Cup finals to date and looked set to continue this sequence after Steve Archibald gave them the lead in the eleventh minute. Liverpool spent most of the game seeking an equaliser but were continually thwarted by Ray Clemence, who had joined Spurs from the Reds the previous summer.

With just three minutes of the game remaining young Irish midfielder Ronnie Whelan, who had only broken into the side two months after the season started at the expense of Ray Kennedy, drove home an equaliser from a David Johnson cross.

Bob Paisley refused to let the players sit down in the break before extra time, a psychological ploy to show Spurs the Reds were ready to keep playing. Eleven minutes into the first period, Whelan fired the ball into the roof of the net from the edge of the six yard box and in the last minute another youngster who had broken into the team that season, Ian Rush, got the third.

It meant Liverpool had become only the second team to retain the League Cup after Nottingham Forest in 1979 and 1980. They were presented with two trophies, with sponsors the *National Dairy Council* donating their own trophy for the competition then known as the Milk Cup.

Liverpool also went onto win the League Championship that season, coincidentally beating Spurs 3-1 in the title clinching game at Anfield after being a goal down at half time. Spurs did taste some success themselves though when they beat Queens Park Rangers in the FA Cup final.

THE MANAGER LIFTS
THE TROPHY

FACT 66

When Liverpool won a third successive League Cup in 1982-83 captain Graeme Souness stood aside to allow outgoing manager Bob Paisley to lift the trophy.

As with the previous season, the Reds had to come from being a goal down at half time to win the cup in extra time. Norman Whiteside gave Manchester United the lead in the twelfth minute only for left back Alan Kennedy to equalise with a low shot from outside the area fifteen minutes from the end of normal time.

In extra time Ronnie Whelan again proved the match winner for Liverpool, scoring with a curling shot eight minutes into the first period and by then the Reds were so dominant in midfield that they should have won by more with substitute David Fairclough missing three good chances.

With manager Bob Paisley having announced his intention to retire at the end of the season and the Reds having been knocked out of the FA Cup the previous month, it was known that this was definitely the outgoing boss's last Wembley visit.

Given the occasion, in a marvellous gesture Souness and the players insisted that Paisley led the side up the 39 steps to the royal box to collect the cup. He did so whilst wearing a grey suit and red scarf and in the knowledge that the Football League Championship trophy was likely to end up at Anfield as well.

1983
CHAMPIONS DESPITE NO WINS IN THE LAST SEVEN GAMES

When Liverpool won a Football League Championship and League Cup double in 1982-83 for the second year running, they did so despite failing to win any of their last league games.

The side that ended the 1981-82 season so strongly after a slow start carried on where they left off, winning five and drawing two of their first seven games. After a wobble in October when they went four games without a win they hit form in November, beginning a sequence of fourteen wins in sixteen games.

A 3-0 win over Swansea City at Anfield on 9th April took them sixteen points clear of second placed Watford, with Manchester United a further four points behind. But the Reds ended up stumbling over the finishing line, drawing 0-0 at Coventry then losing 3-2 at Southampton, where a win would have virtually assured the title given the vastly superior goal difference. However United, who had games in hand due to reaching both the League and FA Cup finals, failed to take advantage of the Reds slip and were beaten 2-0 at Everton on 19th April.

Needing just a point at home to Norwich City on 23rd April, Liverpool lost 2-0, their first home defeat of the season. The following week they lost 2-0 at Tottenham Hotspur but were still confirmed as champions due to United's draw at Norwich. It meant that as with Aston Villa in 1979 and 1980, Spurs had been the opposition in successive years when the Reds were confirmed as Champions.

There were still three games to play, which resulted in a 1-0 defeat at Nottingham Forest, 1-1 home draw with Villa then 2-1 defeat at Watford. Despite the end of season slump, the Reds still finished eleven points clear of Watford.

A FOURTH SUCCESSIVE LEAGUE CUP

FACT 68

When Liverpool won the League Cup in 1983-84 with a historic win over Everton in the final they also made history by becoming the first English team to win a domestic trophy for the fourth successive season.

The Reds needed a replay in every round as well as the final, meaning they played a total of thirteen games compared to only six being needed to win the competition today.

After beating Brentford 8-1 on aggregate in the 2nd round they needed two replays to beat 3rd Division Fulham, then beat Birmingham City and Sheffield Wednesday in replays at Anfield after drawing away. In the semi-finals they were given a favourable draw against 3rd Division Walsall but the Saddlers shocked the Kop by drawing 2-2 at Anfield, only for the Reds to win the second leg 2-0 at Fellows Park.

The final was against Everton, the first of three occasions the Reds and Blues would meet in a Wembley final that decade. They would also twice face each other in Charity Shield games, the first of which had taken place in 1983. It was also the first time two teams from the same city outside London had met in a Wembley final.

In a game most notable for an incident in the first half when Alan Hansen was said by Evertonians to have handled the ball whilst making a clearance, the sides drew 0-0 and went on a joint lap of honour as both sets of fans sang 'Merseyside'. The following Wednesday at Manchester City's Maine Road Graeme Souness scored the only goal of the game to clinch a fourth successive League Cup, a feat that has never been equalled since in any English competition.

A TREBLE SECURED ON OPPOSITION TERRITORY

FACT **69**

Liverpool's fourth European Cup triumph in 1984 saw them become the first club to win the trophy in their opponent's stadium and also completed a treble.

The Reds certainly did things the hard way that season, beating Athletic Bilbao 1-0 away after drawing the first leg 0-0 at Anfield and then winning 4-1 against Benfica in Lisbon after a slender 1-0 home leg win. In the semi-finals they beat Dinamo Bucharest 1-0 at home and 2-1 away to set up a final clash with AS Roma in the Italian club's home ground, the Olympic Stadium.

Phil Neal silenced the crowd with a goal for Liverpool in the fourteenth minute after Dario Bonetti's attempted clearance rebounded into his path off the keeper. A minute before half time Roberto Pruzzo sent the Roma fans wild when he headed the equaliser but the rest of the match was a cagey affair with neither side wanting to push too many men forward.

The game went to penalties and although Steve Nicol missed Liverpool's first, keeper Bruce Grobbelaar wobbled his legs which put off two Roma kickers, causing them to blaze the ball over the bar. Alan Kennedy stepped up to score the winning kick and make Liverpool only the second club, the other being Real Madrid, to win four European Cups.

Liverpool's triumph meant they had completed a treble, making them the first English club to win three trophies in a season, a feat that has only been achieved since by Manchester United in 1999 and the Reds again in 2001.

FACT 70

1986
THE
FORGOTTEN TREBLE

Liverpool famously won the Football League Championship and FA Cup double in 1985-86, beating Everton into second place in both competitions, but they also won a third trophy in a final that was held over to the following season. With English clubs banned from European competition due to the Heysel Stadium disaster, the FA introduced the Screen Sport Super Cup for teams who would otherwise have qualified.

The six sides were divided into two groups of three with the top two in each going through to the semi-finals. It failed to catch the imagination of the public, with Liverpool's two group games against Southampton and Tottenham Hotspur drawing crowds of just 16,189 and 14,855 respectively.

Lack of interest in the competition meant there was no great rush to complete fixtures and the two legs of the Reds semi-final against Norwich City were played three months apart, the second of them four days before the FA Cup final.

The final against Everton was held over to the 1986-87 season and in front of just 20,660 at Anfield, Liverpool won the first leg 3-1 on 16th September. A fortnight later the Reds won 4-1 at a half empty Goodison Park and when captain Alan Hansen collected the cup he showed extremely little enthusiasm for the success.

Although English clubs weren't allowed back into Europe until 1990, this was the first and last time the Super Cup competition was played.

FACT
71

Although Liverpool had to settle for second place in 1986-87 as Everton won the league, there was some consolation for Reds fans when Ian Rush scored his nineteenth Merseyside derby goal, equalling a record that had stood since before the Second World War.

In the summer of 1986 Liverpool sold Rush to Italian giants Juventus for £3.2 million, but he was loaned back to the Reds for the 1986-87 season. Any worries that Rush would simply go through the motions at Anfield were soon dispelled as he went on to score forty goals in all competitions, seven more than in the previous season.

The most memorable goals came on 25th April 1987 against Everton at Anfield, a game the Reds needed to win to keep their fading title hopes alive. Defeat was unthinkable, as it would have put the Blues nine points ahead with three games remaining and a superior goal difference.

Steve McMahon gave the Reds a ninth minute lead but Everton equalised after a quarter of an hour from a Kevin Sheedy free kick. Rush then headed home from close range on the stroke of half time to restore the Reds lead.

In the second half the Reds were kicking towards the Kop but Everton had the better of things and Mike Hooper had to be at his best in goal. Then with five minutes left Kevin Ratcliffe failed to clear a Gary Ablett cross and Rush prodded the ball home to score his nineteenth goal in Merseyside derbies, equalling a record set by Everton's Dixie Dean between 1926 and 1936.

The Kop sang Rush's name for the last five minutes of the game and unknown to them, he would be back at Anfield little over a year later, beating Dean's record in the 1989 FA Cup final.

1988
FOUR
TIMES ELEVEN

Liverpool's Football League Championship winning side of 1987-88 was up there with that from 1978-79 when it came to superlatives.

The Reds moved on seamlessly from the sale of Ian Rush, with the fee received from Juventus being invested in John Barnes and Peter Beardsley, who provided the chances for new goal poacher John Aldridge as well as scoring plenty themselves.

Even a collapsed sewer under the Kop that caused the postponement of the first three home games didn't hinder the Reds as they picked up seven points from their opening three away fixtures.

On 17th October 1987 a 4-0 win over leaders Queens Park Rangers at Anfield took Liverpool top of the table despite having played two games less than everyone else. They were never off the top all season, going 29 games unbeaten from the start which equalled a record that had been set by Leeds United in 1973-74 and was later broken by Arsenal in 2003-04.

Liverpool scored four goals on eleven occasions, most notably on 13th April when Nottingham Forest were hammered 5-0 at Anfield. That performance was described by guest Sir Tom Finney, a legendary former player with Preston North End and England as the finest he had ever seen and one that couldn't be bettered anywhere including Brazil.

The championship was confirmed on 23rd April with a 1-0 home win over Tottenham Hotspur. However the Reds were unable to secure a second double in three years as Wimbledon stunned them by winning 1-0 in the FA Cup final at Wembley with John Aldridge having a penalty saved by Dave Beasant.

1989
CELTIC'S HELPING
HAND TO LIVERPOOL

15th April 1989 will always be the blackest day in Liverpool's history. 95 fans were killed at the FA Cup semi-final in Hillsborough, Sheffield due to overcrowding in the terracing behind the goal. A 96th fan remained in a coma for four years before his life support machine was turned off in 1993.

The club did all it could to help the bereaved and all others affected by the tragedy, opening up the stadium for people to leave flowers and ensuring that every single funeral was attended by players.

When it came to playing again after a period of mourning, Glasgow Celtic came to Liverpool's aid, inviting the Reds to play in a friendly at Celtic Park on 30th April with all proceeds going to the disaster fund.

There was no segregation at the match and before kick off 'You'll Never Walk Alone' was sang with both red and green scarves held aloft all around the ground. After all the stress they had been through, Liverpool's players were glad to be back on the pitch again and won 4-0, with Ian Rush getting two and the others coming from Kenny Dalglish and John Aldridge.

The game had been perfect preparation for the resumption of competitive action, which came the following Wednesday with the Merseyside derby at Goodison Park, which was drawn 0-0.

After much deliberation Liverpool continued playing in the FA Cup at the request of the families of those who died. They beat Everton 3-2 in the final but the league title was snatched from them in the last game of the season when Arsenal won 2-0 at Anfield to win it for themselves.

BOTH LEGS OF CUP TIE AT ANFIELD

FACT **74**

In the 2nd round of the League Cup in 1989-90 Liverpool were drawn to play Wigan Athletic, whose ground was unsuitable for such a high profile fixture leading to both legs being played at Anfield.

Wigan were then in the 3rd Division and played at a ground called Springfield Park, which had had its capacity slashed following the Hillsborough disaster. When it was announced the capacity of the away end would be less than 400, they decided to play their home leg at Anfield to ensure a good crowd, rather than move the game to Wigan's rugby league ground.

In the first game Wigan shocked the Reds by coming back from 1-0 down to go 2-1 up early in the second half. Thankfully for the Reds, two goals from Ian Rush and one each from Peter Beardsley and John Barnes spared their blushes.

For the second leg a fortnight later Wigan were the home team and produced the match programme. In front of a crowd of 17,954, only 1,000 less than for the first leg, they held out for an hour before Liverpool finally found the net through Irish defender Steve Staunton, who had come on as a substitute for Rush at half time.

Despite being a defender Staunton was playing in an advanced role and shocked everybody by going to score two more goals to complete an unlikely hat trick, becoming the first Reds substitute to achieve this feat.

In the following round Liverpool were knocked out by Arsenal, losing 1-0 at Highbury and Wigan have now been regular Premiership visitors to Anfield since 2005, with a smart new stadium to host their own home games.

1990
DALGLISH BECOMES
OLDEST OUTFIELD PLAYER

FACT 75

Liverpool won the Football League Championship for the eighteenth time in 1989-90, with Kenny Dalglish making a cameo appearance in the last game to become the club's oldest outfield player.

The Reds didn't have it all their own way during the season, with Arsenal, Chelsea and Everton all leading the table at some stage during the autumn. Liverpool got better after Christmas, a Boxing Day win over Sheffield Wednesday taking them to the top although they were briefly knocked off by Aston Villa at the end of March.

However Villa lost their nerve, losing three times in a five game spell during April, allowing the Reds to clinch the title with a 2-1 win over Queens Park Rangers with two games remaining.

In their last home game of the season against Derby County on 1st May, the Reds won 1-0 with Gary Gillespie finally breaking the defensive resistance in the 81st minute when he scored from close range after Ronnie Rosenthal's shot had been saved by Peter Shilton.

The biggest cheer up until then had come in the 71st minute when player manager Kenny Dalglish brought himself on for Jan Molby for his first appearance of the season. Despite his age of 39 years and 58 days, which beat Billy Liddell's previous record of 38 years 234 days, Dalglish was soon threading some dangerous passes, although he was letting the ball do as much of the running as he could, as his red face showed.

After the game the players were presented with the championship trophy for the eighteenth time but they have not been able to win it since.

1991
DEAN SAUNDERS FOLLOWS IN FATHER'S FOOTSTEPS

When Liverpool broke the English transfer record and paid £2.9 million for Dean Saunders in the summer of 1991 it meant that for the first time a father and son had represented Liverpool.

Dean's father Roy Saunders came from Salford and signed for the club as a seventeen year old in 1948 but it was five years before he broke into the side. He made 134 appearances at left half (now left midfield), most of them in a three year period in the 2nd Division from 1954-57 before moving on to Swansea in 1959.

His son Dean played for Swansea, Brighton and Hove Albion, Oxford United and Derby County, scoring seventeen goals in 1990-91 as Derby were relegated. Reds boss Graeme Souness, who took over after Kenny Dalglish resigned the previous February, swooped to sign him for a record fee with team mate, defender Mark Wright also arriving at Anfield.

Dean spent only one full season at Anfield, struggling to adapt to a passing style as opposed to Derby's counter attacking play which exploited his pace. His most memorable moments were scoring four against Finnish side Kuuysysi Lahti in a UEFA Cup tie and also netting one against Everton at Anfield. He was then sold to Aston Villa in September 1992, scoring twice in a 4-2 victory for them over the Reds just a week later.

Ironically, 1991 also saw the first known grandson of a former Reds player appear for the club. Defender Rob Jones, who signed from Crewe Alexandra and made his debut at Manchester United on 6th October 1991, was the son of Bill Jones who was part of the 1946-47 title winning side.

1991
BEST
EUROPEAN COMEBACK

In Liverpool's long and illustrious European history, it's amazing that they have only once overturned a two goal first leg deficit to win a European tie, against French side Auxerre in November 1991.

After six years in exile due to the Heysel ban, the Reds returned to Europe in the UEFA Cup and had a comfortable 6-2 aggregate victory in the 1st round against Finnish side Kuuysyi Lahti. Auxerre though were much stronger and the 2-0 scoreline in the first leg in France could have been a lot heavier.

A poor start to the league season had left the Reds ninth in the table after thirteen games and optimism amongst fans wasn't great for this game, especially as an injury crisis led to Graeme Souness naming just four substitutes instead of the usual five. Only 23,094 turned up but those inside the ground created a wall of noise that clearly unsettled the Auxerre players and Liverpool got off to the perfect start when Jan Molby converted a penalty after just four minutes. After Bruce Grobbelaar had made a crucial one on one save from Kovacs, Mike Marsh headed a second on half an hour to level the tie.

In the second half the Reds were kicking into the Kop but they didn't go all out for the third goal, playing a patient game as Auxerre seemed happy to try and take the game to penalties. In the 83rd minute, Mark Walters ran on to a Molby pass to make it 3-0 to send the crowd wild.

Liverpool went on to reach the quarter-finals that season where they were beaten by Genoa and they haven't repeated the feat of overturning a two goal deficit since.

FIRST FA CUP SEMI-FINAL DECIDED BY PENALTIES

FACT 78

In 1992 Liverpool beat 2nd Division Sunderland 2-0 to win the FA Cup final, having been involved in the competition's first semi-final penalty shoot out.

Up until 1990-91, unlimited replays had been used to settle drawn FA Cup ties with the Reds 1980 semi-final with Arsenal not being settled until the third replay. With police now insisting on ten days notice for games the FA announced that penalties would be used after two drawn games and the first shoot-out was in the 1st round in November 1991, Rotherham United beating Scunthorpe United 7-6.

In the semi-final Liverpool were paired with Portsmouth, with the game taking place at Arsenal FC's old stadium Highbury. After a goalless ninety minutes Darren Anderton gave Portsmouth the lead nine minutes from the end of extra time only for Ronnie Whelan to equalise with four minutes left.

The replay took place at Villa Park on 13th April, just two days after Liverpool had played Aston Villa there in a league game. Since the first leg manager Graeme Souness had undergone a major heart operation and Ronnie Moran was acting as caretaker manager.

The game finished 0-0 after extra time after the Reds failed to break down a stubborn Portsmouth defence. In the shoot-out Liverpool's experienced players kept their nerve, going through 3-1 after Portsmouth missed three out of their first four kicks.

1992
THE FIRST TELEVISED
PREMIERSHIP GAME

Liverpool were involved in another television first in 1992, taking part in the first game that was shown on Sky Television which went on to revolutionise the game.

In February 1992 the 1st Division clubs decided to break away from the Football League to form the Premier League, allowing for television money to be split only between the top clubs and not across all four divisions. *British Sky Broadcasting* won the bid for the first television contract, which then was for two games a week, one on the Sunday and another on Monday night. The first game selected was Nottingham Forest versus Liverpool which was played on 16th August 1992.

Keeper David James and midfielder Paul Stewart were making their Reds debuts, but they were beaten 1-0 thanks to a 28th minute goal from Teddy Sheringham and Forest felt they could have won by more.

In what proved to be a startlingly accurate prediction of how Liverpool would go on to perform that season and so many more times in the Premier League era, *The Times* noted that 'Liverpool are not, and perhaps will not be, the formidable side of old'.

Liverpool went on to finish sixth that season while the Premier League, now the Premiership, has been covered on what is now *Sky* ever since, with them showing three games per weekend and one other being shown by a different broadcaster.

1994
SCORER FAILS TO
REMEMBER HIS EQUALISER

In one of the most dramatic comebacks ever seen at Anfield Liverpool came from 3-0 down to draw 3-3 with Manchester United but the scorer of the Reds third goal didn't know anything about it.

Despite a promising start to the season in which the first three games were won, Liverpool suffered a sharp dip in form and were eighth in the table going into this game on 4th January 1994, a massive 21 points behind leaders United.

Steve Bruce headed United into an eighth minute lead and midway through the first half two goals in a three minute spell appeared to put the game beyond the Reds reach. The first was a Ryan Giggs chip from outside the box and second a free kick from Dennis Irwin which gave Bruce Grobbelaar no chance.

In the 25th minute Nigel Clough's low drive gave the Reds hope and in the 38th minute he added another, seizing on a hesitant United defence to fire the ball past Peter Schmeichel. The Reds were then given an almighty let off just before half time when Giggs missed his kick from the edge of the six yard box.

In the second half the Reds were attacking the Anfield Road end and Schmeichel saved a curling Jamie Redknapp shot and long range Stig Bjørnebye effort. In the 79th minute though he could do nothing about Ruddock's header from a Bjørnebye cross. Later Ruddock admitted he had no recollection of the goal or being swamped by his jubilant teammates, having clashed heads with Roy Keane as he rose to meet the ball.

Despite this brilliant comeback, inconsistency would cost Graeme Souness his job three weeks later as the Reds were knocked out of the FA Cup by Bristol City.

1994

FACT 81
A FOUR MINUTE HAT-TRICK IN FRONT OF THE ALL-SEATED KOP

The first home game of 1994-95 against Arsenal saw a teenage striker score a rapid hat-trick in front of the first all seated crowd at Anfield.

The end of 1993-94 saw the demolition of the famous Kop terrace as Liverpool were forced to comply with the requirements of the Taylor Report, which called for all seated stadia following the Hillsborough disaster. In it's place a the current 12,000 seat stand was built, of which 4,000 uncovered seats were ready for the beginning of the new season.

After finishing eighth the previous season and making no major signings in the summer few predicted big things for Liverpool in the coming campaign. But the continuing emergence of Fowler, who was only nineteen and burst onto the scene the previous season before breaking his leg in January, was one of the reasons manager Roy Evans had faith in who was already there.

Fowler's remarkable treble came between the 26th and 31st minutes, the first goal coming when he turned in the rebound after Jamie Redknapp's free kick had bounced into his path. The second came when he collected a pass from Steve McManaman and hit a shot through Lee Dixon's legs that crept in by the post and the third a tap in after his first shot had been save by David Seaman.

Fowler went on to score 31 goals that season and 183 for the Reds overall. Although his hat-trick was a Liverpool and Premiership record, it is not an all time one. That honour stays with Blackburn's John McIntyre who got three in three minutes against Everton in 1922.

1995
LIVERPOOL'S SOUTH LONDON HOME

FACT 82

In 1994-95 Liverpool won the League Cup in Roy Evans's first season in charge, a campaign which included six visits to Crystal Palace FC's Selhurst Park.

The Reds first trip there came on the opening day of the season, when Ian Rush and Steve McManaman scored two each in a 6-1 victory. Palace were sharing their ground with Wimbledon at the time and the Reds were scheduled to play them at Selhurst Park on 28th January, but this match was called off due to a waterlogged pitch about two hours before kick off.

Liverpool were then drawn against Palace in the semi-finals of the League Cup, winning the first leg at Anfield 1-0 on 15th February. But the second leg was rained off, again the decision to postpone the match coming a few hours before kick off.

A week later the Reds were back at Selhurst Park but not for the re-arranged semi-final. This time it was for an FA Cup 5th round replay against Wimbledon, in which John Barnes and Ian Rush scored the goals in a 2-0 win. The following week the Reds were there for the third midweek in succession as the semi-final went ahead, Liverpool winning 1-0 to reach Wembley thanks to Robbie Fowler.

The sixth and final trip to Selhurst Park of the season was on the May Bank Holiday, when Reds fans made up the bulk of the sparse 12,041 crowd who watched a 0-0 draw.

The Reds cup successes at Selhurst Park helped them on their way to a League Cup final against Bolton Wanderers, which was won 2-1 but in the FA Cup they were knocked out in the 6th round by Tottenham Hotspur.

1996
IAN RUSH BREAKS
FA CUP RECORD

When Liverpool cruised to a 7-0 victory against Rochdale in the 3rd round of the FA Cup on 6th January 1996, the goal that was cheered loudest was that scored by Ian Rush, which broke Denis Law's record in the competition.

Liverpool started slowly and didn't score the opening goal until the 21st minute through Robbie Fowler. David James then had to make a few saves from the Rochdale forwards before Stan Collymore struck twice just before half time. Rochdale's day went from bad to worse just three minutes after the restart when Ryan Valentine turned Jason McAteer's cross into his own net. To the 4th Division side's credit though, they never tried to pack their defence and continued to play good football attacking when the opportunity arose.

Rush came on as a substitute just before the hour and it took just three minutes for him to find the net, firing in after a dummy by Fowler. It was his 42nd FA Cup goal, one more than Law (who played for both Manchester clubs in the 1960s and 1970s) and was well received by the Kop, who sang Rush's name as well as some less complimentary chants about Law.

With twenty minutes left Collymore completed his hat trick and McAteer got his first Reds goal five minutes from time. However, all the headlines belonged to Rush, who left the club for Leeds United in the summer and remains Liverpool's all time record scorer. The Reds reached the FA Cup final that season but were beaten 1-0 by Manchester United.

FACT 84
TWO YEARS RUNNING

Liverpool's 4-3 win against Newcastle United in 1996 is often cited as one of the greatest games in that has ever been seen in the Premiership, but the two sides also met eleven months later with the Reds winning by the same scoreline.

Whereas the 1996 game had seen the Reds lead 1-0 then trail 2-1 and 3-2 before finally winning 4-3, the 1997 encounter was much more one sided until the closing stages.

Steve McManaman and Patrik Berger both scored in the space of a minute to give Liverpool the lead after half an hour, with Robbie Fowler hitting a third three minutes before half time. For Kenny Dalglish, who had replaced Kevin Keegan as Newcastle's manager earlier that season, there was then humiliation as a fan ran from the visitors' section of the Anfield Road end and threw a shirt at him.

Liverpool enjoyed plenty of second half possession but were unable to convert it their chances, although even when Keith Gillespie scored for Newcastle in the 71st minute there was little indication of the drama to follow.

With three minutes left Jamie Redknapp lost possession to Faustino Asprilla who lobbed David James, then a minute later James failed to gather the ball properly and when it broke loose Warren Barton bundled the ball over the line.

There was still time for one last twist however as in injury time Stig Bjørnebye crossed from the left and Fowler rose to head the ball past Shaka Hislop to the delight of the Kop.

1997
YOUNGEST
GOALSCORER

Michael Owen became Liverpool's youngest scorer when he struck his first goal for the club on 6th May 1997 but it wasn't enough to keep Liverpool in the title race.

The Reds travelled to Selhurst Park to face Wimbledon knowing that they needed a win to keep their fading title hopes alive. Although the majority of the 20,016 crowd were backing the Reds, the players failed to respond in the first half and Wimbledon's opener after 43 minutes was fully deserved.

After eleven minutes of the second half Dean Holdsworth headed the home side 2-0 ahead, leading to Owen, who was just 17 years and 143 days old, to come off the bench. With sixteen minutes left he had pulled one back for Liverpool but although this led to their best spell of the game, with Owen forcing a diving save from keeper Neil Sullivan, no equaliser was forthcoming.

The defeat meant that the Reds now trailed Manchester United by four points with one game remaining, confirming the Old Trafford club as champions for the second year running.

Within a year Owen had also become England's youngest scorer and gained worldwide recognition when he scored a wonder goal against Argentina in the World Cup. He went on to score 158 goals for Liverpool before moving to Real Madrid in 2004.

1998
LIVERPOOL BEAT
EIGHT MEN

One of Liverpool's most bizarre games was on 28th March 1998, when the Reds beat Barnsley 3-2 at Oakwell, thanks to an injury time goal in a game that saw three Barnsley players sent off.

Relegation threatened Barnsley had already shocked the Reds, winning 1-0 at Anfield earlier in the season. A surprise again looked possible in the 37th minute when Neil Redfearn put Barnsley ahead but shortly before half time Karl Heinz Riedle equalised for Liverpool.

Soon after the start of the second half, Michael Owen was clean through on goal and was tripped by Darren Barnard who was red carded. Riedle then hit an excellent goal from thirty yards to put the Reds 2-1 up on the hour. Soon afterwards Barnsley were reduced to nine men when Chris Morgan was sent off for an incident that saw Owen fall to the ground clutching his face.

Despite having a two man advantage, Liverpool struggled to cope with Barnsley substitute Georgi Hristov, who forced two good saves from David James before being brought down in the box by Phil Babb with five minutes remaining, leading to a penalty being awarded.

Redfearn sent James the wrong way with the penalty but there was still more drama to come when Liverpool were awarded a free kick in injury time. It was taken quickly and Steve McManaman restored Liverpool's lead, to the anger of Barnsley players who weren't ready. During their arguments with the referee Darren Sheridan was sent off meaning they finished the game with eight men.

The Reds near failure to win the game showed up many of the inconsistencies of Roy Evans's management and at the end of the season Gerard Houllier arrived to take joint control.

FACT **87**

Liverpool's biggest win in any competition came on 29th November 2000 when they beat Stoke City 8-0 at the Britannia Stadium in a League Cup 4th round tie.

The game could have been so different though had Stoke forward Peter Thorne not missed a sitter in the fourth minute. After chasing a backpass he dispossessed Reds keeper Pegguy Arphexad only to see his shot hit the post.

Liverpool were ahead two minutes after Thorne's miss, Christian Ziege scoring from close range but for the next twenty minutes Stoke did all they could to find an equaliser. However two goals in three minutes from Vladimír Šmicer and Markus Babbel just before the half hour put Liverpool in total control. Robbie Fowler headed in a corner in the 39th minute to give the Reds a 4-0 half time lead.

After 59 minutes Sami Hyppia scored the fifth and the sixth came from Danny Murphy on 65 minutes, both goals coming in the total absence of home defenders. With eight minutes remaining Fowler was set up by Ziege to make it 7-0 and two minutes later scored from a penalty. By then the scoreboard operator had lost count and displayed the score as 9-0, but there was no further scoring and the final goals total remained at eight.

Liverpool went on to win the League Cup that season beating Birmingham City on penalties in the final, the first step of a memorable cup treble from a side now solely managed by Gerard Houllier.

2001
PEPE PLAYS AGAINST
REDS AT ANFIELD

Liverpool won their third UEFA Cup in 2001 beating Alaves 5-4 in a memorable final in Dortmund. On their way to the final though, they came up against a young Pepe Reina, who was playing for Barcelona when they faced the Reds in the semi-final.

Although it's widely known Reina had joined Liverpool from Villareal in 2005, few realise he spent his early career at Barcelona, where injuries to both first and second choice keepers gave him a run in the side in 2000-01.

Reina was just eighteen and had a full head of hair when Barcelona reached the semi-final of the UEFA Cup, where the sides met at Anfield in the second leg after a 0-0 draw in the Nou Camp.

Liverpool's Sander Westerveld was the busier of the two keepers early on, touching over a dipping drive from Rivaldo and seeing a Luis Enrique low shot going just wide of the post. However in the 44th minute Patrick Kluivert handled a corner and Gary McAllister hit the resultant penalty low to Reina's left to give Liverpool the lead.

In the second half the Kop did all they could to help Liverpool to the final, Houllier joking that they scared Barcelona away from the goal. Reina denied Michael Owen on a couple of occasions and wrote of his Anfield experience in his autobiography, "I came away thinking that it was a special place to play football and I wanted to go back there." Four years later he did.

Liverpool's win in the final in Dortmund was the third cup triumph of the season, making them the only English team to win the League Cup, FA Cup and a European trophy in the same season.

2001
THE
FOURTH FINAL

Although 2000-01 saw Liverpool win three cups, the final league game of the season that saw them qualify for the Champions League for the first time was seen by many as just as important.

Liverpool visited The Valley to face Charlton Athletic three days after the gruelling UEFA Cup final with Alaves which was settled in extra time. The previous season they had lost 1-0 at relegation threatened Bradford City on the last day to be denied a Champions League place and Gerard Houllier admitted failing to qualify this time would be a major disappointment despite the triple cup success.

With many of his players exhausted, Houllier took a gamble and made four changes to the side that had played in Dortmund for a game Liverpool needed to win to be certain of qualification. However in the first half this still failed to inspire the side, who looked jaded and were second to every ball as well as being overrun in midfield. Only the brilliant goalkeeping of Sander Westerveld and the post kept the Reds in the game at half time.

In the second half Liverpool were a different side and ten minutes after the restart Robbie Fowler scored a superb overhead kick to make it 1-0. Danny Murphy came off the bench to make it 2-0 after an hour and when Fowler got his second with twenty minutes to go qualification was assured. Michael Owen completed an emphatic second half, scoring the fourth with ten minutes left.

The win completed a remarkable end to the season for the Reds, who in addition to their cup exploits had won eight of their last nine games to clinch the Champions League spot which had looked beyond them after closest rivals Leeds United won 2-1 at Anfield on Good Friday.

2002
LIVERPOOL INVITED TO
REAL MADRID CENTENARY

In 2002 Liverpool were one of four clubs, including the hosts Real Madrid, who took part in a special tournament at the Bernabeu Stadium to celebrate the centenary of the Spanish giants.

Real Madrid traditionally host a prestigious pre-season friendly at which the winners are presented with the Trofeo Santiago Bernabeu. Due to this being their centenary year, it was decided to host a tournament to which four of the most successful clubs in European Cup/Champions League history were invited.

The tournament was played over three days and kicked off on the Friday night with a game between Real Madrid and Liverpool. Real, who three months earlier had won the Champions League by beating Bayer Leverkusen 2-1 at Hampden Park, won 2-0 to repeat the scoreline of 1989 when they and the Reds had met to contest the Trofeo Santiago Bernabeu. The following day Bayern Munich beat AC Milan 2-1 to decide the line-up for the final and 3rd placed play off which both took place on the Sunday.

In the 3rd placed play off Liverpool beat AC Milan 2-1, the Reds goals coming from an own goal by Dario Šimić and Milan Baros. Bayern Munich then upset the centenary celebrations by beating Real Madrid 2-1 in the final.

SIX WINNERS MEDALS
IN SIX GAMES

FACT 91

When Liverpool beat Manchester United 2-0 in the final of the League Cup in 2002-03 it earned keeper Pegguy Arphexad his sixth winners medal, meaning he had played as many games as he had medals for the Reds.

Arphexad, who comes from the Caribbean island of Guadeloupe, had signed for the club in 2000 as cover for Sander Westerveld and was an unused substitute in all three finals in 2001. He was also on the bench for the Charity Shield and European Super Cup final early the next season meaning he picked up five winners medals that year.

By 2002-03 he was third choice behind both Jerzy Dudek and Chris Kirkland but an injury to Kirkland meant he was on the bench for this final. Steven Gerrard gave the Reds a 39th minute lead and the Dudek then put in a brilliant performance to keep United at bay before Michael Owen sealed the victory in four minutes from time with a breakaway goal.

The victory meant Liverpool had now won a record sixth League Cup and Arphexad had six medals, having only played six games in three seasons for the Reds, the last of them when he came on as a substitute at Ipswich in February 2002 when Westerveld got injured.

The following summer he signed for Coventry City but was sent on loan to Notts County and after spending a season with Marseille as a back up keeper he has drifted out of the game.

2004
FIRST AWAY COMEBACK
FOR 23 YEARS

When Liverpool beat Fulham 4-2 at Craven Cottage on 16th October 2004 it was the first time they had been losing an away match at half time and went on to win the game since 1991.

The Reds had made an inconsistent start under new manager Rafael Benitez and the first half was woeful to watch. They rarely put more than two passes together and lost possession too easily, and could have no complaints about being 2-0 down at the break.

At half time Benitez made a substitution that changed the game, taking off Salif Diao and sending on Xabi Alonso. Within three minutes they had pulled a goal back thanks to a piece of good fortune, a Milan Baros shot deflecting off Zat Knight and deceiving the keeper. In the 71st minute they levelled when Baros scored from close range after Luis Garcia's header had been saved.

A few minutes after equalising the Reds suffered a blow when Josemi was sent off for a second yellow card but they did not seek to grind out a draw with ten men. Instead they went for victory. In the 79th minute they took the lead from an Alonso free kick that gave Edwin Van Der Sar no chance. The Reds suffered a scare two minutes from time when Papa Diop was through on goal but his weak shot was saved by Chris Kirkland. Igor Biscan then scored a fourth in injury time with a curling shot after a one-two with Stephen Warnock.

The last time Liverpool had been losing at half time away from home and won the match was against Notts County in 1991-92. This victory showed that although lacking in complete quality, Benitez's team had a fighting spirit. Something that ensured success when they achieved Champions League glory at the end of the season.

2005
LIVERPOOL FINISH FINAL DAY AFTER IT STARTED

25th May 2005 will forever remain in history as the date Liverpool staged one of the greatest comebacks in history to become champions of Europe for the fifth time, but the game actually came to a conclusion on the 26th.

Despite only finishing fifth in the league, Liverpool exceeded all expectations in only their third Champions League campaign, achieving memorable victories over Juventus and Chelsea to reach the final against AC Milan in Istanbul.

The Reds couldn't have got off to a worse start when Paulo Maldini put Milan ahead in the first minute but despite the next 35 minutes being evenly matched two Milan goals in the last six minutes of the first half put them in a commanding position.

The second half initially seemed to be a case of avoiding a humiliating scoreline and even when Steven Gerrard made it 3-1 on 54 minutes a comeback seemed improbable. But when Vladimír Šmicer's speculative drive deceived Milan keeper Dida two minutes later the whole atmosphere changed and as Liverpool surged forward after an equaliser, Milan Baros was felled in the box and a penalty awarded. Xabi Alonso's kick was saved but he scored from the rebound and Liverpool's comeback was complete in what Milan coach Carlo Ancellotti described as 'six minutes of madness'

There was no further scoring and the game went to penalties, Jerzy Dudek saving two of Milan's kicks as the Reds triumphed 3-2. The only Reds player who had scored in the match that took a kick in the shoot-out was Šmicer who converted his penalty after midnight giving him the rare distinction of scoring twice in the same match but on different days.

2006
REDS WIN LAST
CARDIFF CUP FINAL

Between 2001 and 2006 six FA Cup finals were played in Cardiff due to the re-building of Wembley Stadium, with Liverpool winning the first and last of them.

The Reds beat Arsenal 2-1 in the first Cardiff FA Cup final in 2001 but didn't reach the final again until 2006, when they were involved in one of the most exciting finals for years against West Ham United.

After 21 minutes in Cardiff, West Ham went ahead despite not having any shots at goal, when Jamie Carragher bundled a Lionel Scaloni cross into his own net. Seven minutes later Dean Ashton made it 2-0 after Pepe Reina had failed to hold a Matthew Etherington shot, but Djibril Cisse's volley in the 32nd minute got Liverpool right back in the game.

Steven Gerrard equalised for Liverpool in the ninth minute of the second half, smashing in an unstoppable shot from a Peter Crouch knock down. With 25 minutes remaining though, a mis-hit cross from Paul Konchesky deceived Reina and restored West Ham's lead. The cup looked to be going to West Ham but in injury time Gerrard levelled the scores, firing in from thirty yards after the Hammers could only half clear the ball.

In extra time both sides were tired but West Ham came closest to scoring when Nigel Reo Coker's header was tipped onto the post by Reina. When it rebounded to Marlon Harewood he hit the ball wide when it appeared easier to score. In the penalty shoot-out Reina, who had been at fault for the second and third West Ham goals, made amends by saving three kicks. The crucial save came from West Ham's fourth kick, taken by Anton Ferdinand, which gave the Reds the FA Cup for the seventh time.

REDS SET CHAMPIONS LEAGUE SCORING RECORD

FACT 95

After a slow start to their 2007-08 Champions League campaign Liverpool finally got a win in their fourth group game against Besiktas, setting a new highest victory record in the process.

Liverpool had drawn one and lost two of their first three games, which included a 2-1 defeat to Besiktas in Istanbul. Failure to win this game would leave the Reds requiring an unlikely combination of results to take the Reds to the knockout stage.

Besiktas were missing their star defender Gokhan Zan but that should still not have made it so easy for the Reds, who went 1-0 up through Peter Crouch in the nineteenth minute when he took advantage of a poor clearance. Just after the half hour Yossi Benayoun got the Reds second with a low drive and the score remained 2-0 at half time.

Within eleven minutes of the restart Benayoun had completed a hat-trick with two goals in a four minute spell, first scoring from the rebound after John Arne Riise's shot was saved and then doing the same after Steven Gerrard's free kick wasn't held by the keeper.

Gerrard got Liverpool's fifth with a well taken goal after a one-two, then Ryan Babbel's clever back heel made it 6-0 with twelve minutes to go. Babbel's second was a comical goal and summed up Besiktas's night, as he charged down an Ibrahim Toraman clearance and it looped high over the keeper into the net. Crouch, who had started the rout, completed it with a minute to go.

The 8-0 win beat the previous record of 7-0, jointly held by Juventus and Arsenal. Liverpool won their next two games to get out of the group, eventually reaching the semi-finals where they were beaten by Chelsea.

LIVERPOOL CHANGE
REAL MADRID PHILOSOPHY

FACT 96

Liverpool's victory over Real Madrid in the Champions League round of 16 in 2009 helped shape the Spanish giants' transfer policy.

The Reds won the first leg 1-0 in the Bernabeu Stadium thanks to a headed goal from Yossi Benayoun. Then in the second leg at Anfield the rest of Europe was stunned by the emphatic nature of Liverpool's 4-0 victory, which could have been far more had it not been for some poor finishing and the great goalkeeping of Iker Casillas.

The defeat was Real Madrid's worst in Europe since they lost 5-0 against AC Milan in 1988-89 and made worse by the fact their great rivals Barcelona were progressing well and would win Europe's biggest prize for only the third time that season.

At the end of the season a new President was elected at Real Madrid. Florentino Perez had held the position from 2000 to 2006 when he followed a policy of signing Galacticos – big name players for massive fees. Amongst those signed were Zinedine Zidane, Roberto Carlos and David Beckham, but the policy arguably didn't work too well as no trophies were won between 2004 and 2006.

Perez was succeeded by Ramon Calderon and although Real Madrid won the title in 2007 and 2008, their supporters craved the Champions League and Perez was re-elected in 2009. The defeat to Liverpool had played a large part in the supporters voting for Perez and he promised a return to the Galactico's policy, buying Kaka from AC Milan and breaking the world transfer record to sign Christiano Ronaldo for £80 million from Manchester United.

Real Madrid didn't forget the quality of some of Liverpool's players either, buying Xabi Alonso and Alvaro Arbeloa from the Reds that summer.

2010
FIRST TROPHYLESS
MANAGER FOR FIFTY YEARS

Roy Hodgson's brief spell as manager in 2010-11 ended after just six months in charge, making him the first Liverpool manager to fail to win a trophy since Phil Taylor who was in charge from 1956 to 1959.

After finishing a disappointing seventh in 2009-10, one year after pushing Manchester United all the way for the title, Rafael Benitez left by mutual consent. Despite calls by many for the return of Kenny Dalglish who was now involved in the club's Academy, Hodgson was appointed after guiding Fulham to the Europa League final knocking out holders Shakhtar Donetsk and Juventus on the way.

Things may have turned out far differently for Hodgson and the Reds had Pepe Reina not conceded a last minute own goal against Arsenal on the opening day of the season. Liverpool had been down to ten men since Joe Cole was sent off just before half time but had still taken the lead early in the second half through David Ngog only to be forced to settle for a draw.

After that results were extremely disappointing with the Reds winning only one of the opening eight games and a 2-0 defeat at Everton on 17th October left them second bottom of the table. Although results improved by Christmas they were still only ninth and a 1-0 home defeat to struggling Woverhampton Wanderers in the last game of 2010 saw the crowd turn against Hodgson. There was also humiliation in the League Cup, with League Two side Northampton winning on penalties at Anfield after a 2-2 draw.

A 3-1 defeat at Blackburn Rovers on 5th January 2011 marked the end of Hodgson's short spell in charge and Dalglish took over the manager's role, with Hodgson later being appointed by West Bromwich Albion and then England.

2011
ENGLISH LEAGUE
FOOTBALL'S LATEST GOAL

On 17th April 2011 Liverpool drew 1-1 at Arsenal with Dirk Kuyt's injury time penalty being the latest goal recorded in both the Football League and Premiership in 123 years.

The game was delayed during the second half when Jamie Carragher suffered from concussion, leading to eight minutes of stoppage time being added. In the final minute of this Jay Spearing fouled Cesc Fàbregas in the box and Robin Van Persie scored the penalty, which looked certain to have won the game for Arsenal.

Despite time being up, the delay caused by the penalty meant the referee allowed play to go on and after 100 minutes of the game Liverpool were awarded a free kick on the edge of the box. Steven Gerrard took this and appealed for a penalty as he believed it was blocked by a hand. The referee waved this away but Lucas was then bundled over by Emmauel Eboué as he chased the ball.

Dirk Kuyt stepped up to take the kick which struck the back of the net as the clock ticked towards 112 minutes having been played. It was the latest goal ever recorded since the Football League was founded in 1888.

Liverpool's League Cup win in 2012 bore some similarities with previous triumphs in the same competition, especially 1981:- In 2012 Liverpool beat Manchester City in the semi-final to reach the final, winning 1-0 away and then drawing 2-2 at Anfield. In 1981 the Reds beat City in the semi-final, winning the away leg 1-0 before drawing the home leg, although on that occasion it was 1-1.

In 2012 Liverpool were playing a team from football's second tier in the final and conceded a late goal, with Cardiff's equaliser that forced penalties coming in the 118th minute. In 1981 Liverpool played 2nd Division West Ham United and looked set to win the cup after Alan Kennedy gave them a 1-0 extra time lead, only for Ray Stewart to equalise with a penalty in the 120th minute to force a replay.

In 2012 Liverpool won the League Cup and West Ham United were promoted from the Championship and Charlton Athletic from League One. In 1981 West Ham were promoted from the 2nd Division and Charlton from the 3rd Division, which were then the second and third tiers.

In addition to the similarities with 1981:- In 2012 Liverpool beat Exeter City and Stoke City on their way to winning the competition. They had beaten those sides on the way to previous finals in 1982 and 2001 respectively in exactly the same rounds.

In 2012 Liverpool beat a team in the final who then lost out on promotion to the Premiership via the play offs. In 2001 Liverpool beat Birmingham in the final, who then lost to Preston in the play offs.

2012
DERBY CUP SEMI-FINAL JINX STRIKES AGAIN

When Liverpool lost the 2012 FA Cup final 2-1 to Chelsea, it continued the 100% record of the Reds going on to lose the final whenever they had beaten Everton in the semi-final.

Just three weeks after beating Everton 2-1 at Wembley in the semi-final, Liverpool were back at the stadium where they lost 2-1 to Chelsea. It's an interesting fact that on the three occasions when Liverpool have played a London club at Wembley after beating Everton in the semi-final, they have gone on to lose by the same scoreline they had won the semi-final. The other two occasions were both against Arsenal, in 1950 and 1971.

The fourth occasion when the Reds have beaten Everton in an FA Cup semi-final was in 1977, when they won a replay 3-0 at Maine Road after a 2-2 draw. They then went on to lose the final 2-1 against Manchester United.

On the other hand, when Everton have beaten Liverpool in the semi-final, they have gone on to win the cup, although this has only happened once, in 1906. That year Everton won 2-0 at Villa Park, then won the cup by beating Newcastle United 1-0 at Crystal Palace. Liverpool did have the consolation of finishing the season as League Champions however.

The 100 Facts Series